# An Easter Heart

## A STORY OF BELIEF

*A devotional*

JENNIFER JACKSON

# An Easter Heart

## A STORY OF BELIEF

*A devotional*

Edited by Ali Hooper; www.alihooper.com
Cover and interior design by Kreativity Inc.; www.kreativityinc.com

# Table of Contents

# Introduction

My dream is that this devotional will be a spot of joy and inspiration to you in the days leading up to Easter. I hope that you will take a little time each day or week to read a chapter, and then spend some time in your journal reflecting, praying and applying the truths that you have learned. Perhaps you want to gather one, two or more best girlfriends to read and reflect together. Everything is better in community.

The recipes are for you to savor but also an invitation to worship the Lord by singing in the kitchen while planning to celebrate Him with family and friends. After such a long season of isolation, Spring will be here again soon. Buy some flowers, set a pretty table, bake a cake and prepare a meal for those you love. In the Bible they fasted and feasted. Perhaps you will fast in some fashion for the 40 days of Lent to settle your heart, your Easter believing heart, and then enjoy the most special holiday by going all out in honor of the cross and resurrection.

Finally, this devotional was never intended for simple enjoyment. While I hope you do enjoy reading through it, my prayer is that it cultivates in you a richer and deeper faith and a greater experience of Jesus. Each chapter incorporates a variety of action steps for you to take in the hopes that your Easter heart will soften, expand and grow. Invite others to join you, and together experience the fullness of a life alongside Jesus, our living hope.

# Dedication

This book is for my two incredible daughter-n-loves, Misti and Brandi.

I had always hoped for a girl but soon realized that only boys were God's plan for me. Embracing life as a boy mom, I began to pray for their future wives from the time my boys were very small. God knew how important their future wives would be to our lives, and He answered in the most tremendous way!

You are both women of strength and compassion, courage and joy, dedication and discipline, love and grace. I look forward to all the meals, shopping, laughing, farm and spa days that lie ahead for all of us! To say I am proud of you would be an understatement. My heart beams and overflows with gratitude.

# Acknowledgements

Special thanks to Rachel Patton and Elaine Bartels, you have always provided me with recipes, canning, entertaining and cooking tips over the years. You are both the best!

Thanks to Allen Jackson, my brother-n-law, for always providing wisdom around the table and especially good, delicious centerpieces.

Thanks to my mom, Sherrie Godbey, for making every meal taste great and feel like home.

Thanks to my precious mother-n-law, Betty Jackson, for teaching me how to make homemade bread. I only wish we had room to print the wheat roll recipe!

Alison "Ali" Hooper - You are beyond measure! It's rare to find someone that you instantly have a special connection with, but we certainly do. Your work ethic matches mine, but most importantly your heart for Jesus and people shines through. You are upbeat, fun and talented yet overflowing with love for God. Thanks for looking into all my typos and errors because everything you touch just flows better and makes sense. Go team! You have encouraged, cheered, and prodded me all along the way. Thank you!

Ann-Michel "Chel" Kissler - Amidst your full household of busy kids I have no idea how you create such beautiful graphics, but you do. This book is as lovely and graceful as you live your life. The prayers poured out for me, the joy given, the times of friendship and tea have been gifts all along the way. From the bottom of my heart, thank you; those words just don't seem big enough.

# Forward

When I was a young boy, God brought someone into my life who would forever change my fate. Though she was petite in stature, this visitor was a force for Jesus. She had been a missionary in Cuba but was asked to leave the country because of "the revolution." When she arrived at our house, she was fully devoted to the gospel and sharing with others the good news of Jesus.

One of her first discoveries was that little Doyle (that was me) needed discipline. Even at a very young age, I had a strong will. She could see that what I needed was to surrender my life to the love of God through Jesus. She taught my parents how to lovingly correct, discipline and train my young heart. She understood the cross of Jesus Christ like few people I have ever known. She taught my entire family that Jesus went to the cross not only to save us from our sins but also so that we might experience complete freedom through Him. The discipline that I began to receive combined with the salvation I found in Jesus transformed my life.

When I read through the pages of Jennifer's book, *An Easter Heart*, I can hear the voice of my small but mighty Aunt Mary. I could feel the presence of Jesus when Aunt Mary visited our home, and I can feel the presence of Jesus throughout the pages of this book.

So many people dress up for Easter, attend a church service and then return to life as they knew it. Why settle for such a limited experience when you can experience complete and eternal freedom through an ongoing relationship with Jesus? Jennifer and I have spent the last (almost) 30 years of our lives challenging friends, neighbors and anyone who would listen to draw closer to God and experience that complete freedom.

If you are ready for that kind of experience with the true and living God, then this devotional will serve you as a wonderful and practical guide. I encourage you to do more than simply turn its pages. Get out your Bible, a pen and a notebook, and use this devotional to help you roll away the stone and receive the Easter heart that God intended for you to have.

If you are a man and happened to open this, I encourage you to read on. It may be written from Jennifer's perspective, but I was there. These are the lessons we have learned, shared and taught together, over and over again.

There are two ways to learn a lesson. 1) Make mistakes and hopefully learn from your mistakes, and 2) Let someone else make the mistake and hopefully learn from them. What if you could learn from us? What if you could bypass some of the pain from making the mistakes yourself? This is why Jennifer and I teach, write and share. Humble yourself, choose to be a learner and reap the benefits of that growth. Not only will you discover hope and peace, but in doing so, you will be a conduit of that hope and peace to your family, friends, community, church and so many more.

This book has been fun for me because through it I have relived the romance and fun that Jennifer and I have experienced throughout our life together. We have been blessed by our many trips to Jerusalem, even spending seasons of our life living there. I see the streets, smell the bread and spices, taste the flavors and hear the sounds from the shops of the Old City. Jesus walked some of the exact same stones and hills that Jennifer shares with you throughout these pages, and now you will get to walk them with us.

I'm as excited for you as I was when I took Jennifer to Jerusalem for the first time. It reminds me of the times on the farm that Aunt Mary would take my hand and walk with me, teaching me about Jesus along the way.

Let's walk with Him together.

"He (Jesus) himself bore our sin" in his body on the cross, so that we might die to sin and live for righteousness; "by his wounds you have been healed." For "you were like sheep going astray," but now you have returned to the Shepherd and Overseer of your souls (1 Peter 2:24-25).

Doyle Jackson
*January, 2021*

START WITH A QUICK
SENTENCE PRAYER

———

*Lord, I choose to humble myself before you.*

# The Entry

## A HUMBLE HEART

We started at the top of the Mount of Olives. It was 90 degrees with a light breeze of Mediterranean air, a weather combination that I love. We walked along a steep and winding road overlooking Jerusalem in all her glory. I could see the gate where Peter and John prayed for the lame man to rise and walk, and I could see the thousands of graves where loved ones placed stones to remind them of their grief. I thought to myself, "Jesus will return here one day, and all of these dead bones will rise." I reached out, grabbed Doyle's hand and whispered, This is the holy land.

As I passed a camel and other weary travelers, my mind wandered from what this land will one day hold to what this hill was like in Jesus' day.

As the scriptures promised, Jesus was ready for His Palm Sunday parade. "Do not be afraid, Daughter Zion; see, your king is coming, seated on a donkey's colt" (John 12:15).

INSTEAD OF YOUR SHAME YOU WILL RECEIVE A DOUBLE PORTION, AND INSTEAD OF DISGRACE YOU WILL REJOICE IN YOUR INHERITANCE. AND SO YOU WILL INHERIT A DOUBLE PORTION IN YOUR LAND, AND EVERLASTING JOY WILL BE YOURS.

*Isaiah 61:7*

Sitting humbly on a borrowed donkey, Jesus was surrounded by a crowd. In only a few short days He would be nailed to a cross, and some of those who surrounded Him in the crowd would soon be His betrayers, mockers and attackers. Yet there on that donkey, Jesus smiled with a heart full of love and compassion for the people who lined the streets and placed branches and coats across the dusty, rocky road. Each coat reflected its unique owner and their finest treasure, a symbol of their identity or position. Poor or wealthy, the coats bowed low, stripping away the grip of pride to make a path for the humble King. The faithful, the hopeful, the doubting and the wondering - young and old - they all shouted His name, waved their palm branches and cheered,

*"Hosanna, Glory To God! King of Kings!"*

I imagined how Jesus must have felt. Tears welled up in His eyes and a lump filled His throat. In that moment, Jesus, both fully human and fully divine, wept.

As I walked that same still dusty, rocky

AS HE APPROACHED JERUSALEM AND SAW THE CITY, HE WEPT OVER IT AND SAID, "IF YOU, EVEN YOU, HAD ONLY KNOWN ON THIS DAY WHAT WOULD BRING YOU PEACE - BUT NOW IT IS HIDDEN FROM YOUR EYES."
*Luke 19:41-42*

road where Jesus traveled through the crowd on a donkey, I pondered the words, "Jesus wept."

"AS HE APPROACHED JERUSALEM AND SAW THE CITY, HE WEPT OVER IT" (LUKE 19:41).

Drowning out the sound of my friends and the tour guide, the words Jesus wept rang in my ears over and over again. As they did, we stopped at my absolute most favorite spot in all of Israel. I know that many people love the Sea of Galilee, the Stations of the Cross or the Wailing Wall, but for me, it's the Dominus Flevit Church. This church was fashioned in the shape of a teardrop to symbolize the tears of Christ. In Latin, Dominus Flevit translates as "The Lord wept."

Happy to find a hiding place, I snuck inside the small one-room chapel shaped like a teardrop. Inside there is only a kneeling bench and a small window overlooking the city. All alone, I became emotional as I thought about Jesus who wept during His entry into Jerusalem. He wept, but why?

I began to wonder, did Jesus weep because some in the crowd lacked faith? Was it because some didn't even recognize who He was? Was it because He knew of the great price He would pay for their sins? If only they knew and if only they believed, then they would have the gift of life that would last for eternity.

Was He missing heaven and His Father? Was He thinking about the beautiful home He had prepared for them? Maybe He cried because He knew how things would soon change. Maybe He cried because of how much He would miss fellowship with Peter and James and the rest of His disciples.

What if He wept because He knew how they would grieve? He knew the price they too would pay so that others might know Him.

As I wondered about His weeping, I wondered about my own heart. Can I ever find space in my heart to open up to Father God like Jesus did? Can I ever find a believing Easter heart that weeps with such humility, compassion and love?

---

JESUS' COMPASSION FOR THEM - FOR
BOTH THE CROWD AND THE CITY,
BROUGHT HIM TO TEARS.

---

He rode humbly into Jerusalem with tears of compassion streaming down His face. He wept for those who believed, and He wept for those who did not. He came that we might believe, and He came with deep compassion. We too must soften our hearts for those around us. Allow His compassion to spread to those in our families, our communities and our cities, that they might know this humble, weeping Savior who loves with such agonizing compassion.

Kneeling inside the little dome, tear-shaped room in my most favorite place in the most holy land, I began to cry, and I began to pray. "Father, I cry before you today. I cry because my past mistakes are weighing me down." I began to name my sins one by one before Him like a scrolling list... my harsh words, unkindness and selfish ways. "God, will you take them?" Tears fell harder and turned into full sobs as I realized all that I needed to repent and change and all that He had done for me. I needed to let go. I wanted my tears to wash away my stains.

My prayer continued, "I desire to be close to you, Lord, and learn how to tell you everything, both the good and the bad. I weep because I need my cold heart to soften and be compassionate like yours. Break my heart, Lord, for those wandering, hurting and lost. Help me to see them the way you do and to respond in love." I began to feel a shift in my heart, and in that moment, God did answer me. I began to sense a strange new love for people, my city and my family. Their names and dozens of faces came before my mind. It all bubbled up in me, and I wept for them with Him.

*I wept for them with Him.*

The tour guide called, "Come on, we must keep going," and I was jolted from my prayerful weeping. My heart longed to stay, and I prayed, "Oh, but Jesus, I just want to kneel here in the church of your weeping. I want to weep with you over the lost ones in my life and the lack of faith in my own. I want to lay down my coat and wave my branch in praise. Please keep going on your Palm Sunday ride because we need the cross that you face."

Only a few days before His triumphal entry into Jerusalem, Jesus spent time with His friends. Different people came in and out to meet Him, speak with Him or dine with Him. In the midst of the happiness and fellowship, Mary, Lazarus' sister, arrived to anoint Jesus for burial.

I imagine that she felt the weight of the cross before Him though she could not have known all that He would soon endure. All she knew was that her life had been changed by His presence. She was overflowing with gratitude for the healing and wholeness He had brought into her life. Overwhelmed by love, she found her most valuable possession, a jar of perfume, worth her entire salary for a year. She didn't count the cost or maybe she counted every penny, but regardless, she spent it all for Him. She literally poured it all out. Her tears mixed with care, and her hair wiped her appreciation all over His feet.

---

HER TEARS MIXED WITH CARE, AND
HER HAIR WIPED HER APPRECIATION
ALL OVER HIS FEET

---

No one understood what was happening, but she continued anointing Jesus with her jar of perfume, gaining boldness in her task. As she did, she wept. I imagine how every tear represented a regret, an abuse or a tough place through which she had walked. Her tears cleansed her, and as they flowed, so did forgiveness. With her head down, she washed the dirt from where He would soon be scarred, and He washed her broken dreams. All the "unforgivables" were washed away and gone.

"The Spirit of the Sovereign Lord is on me, because the Lord has anointed me to proclaim good news to the poor. He has sent me to bind up the brokenhearted, to proclaim freedom for the captives and release from darkness for the prisoners" (Isaiah 61:1).

Chemists say that our sense of smell is the strongest sense for memory. The smell of perfume sealed hope in Mary's heart. Like the coats that the crowd laid down before Jesus as He entered Jerusalem, she poured out her perfume upon her precious Savior. Maybe she once wore it to cover up the stench of her life, but now it would be the sweet memory of a special day of tears at Jesus' feet. Oblivious to the others in the room, she was not ashamed to show her true heart, an Easter heart. She believed. As she surrendered her heart and tears she was changed. As she poured the oil, He was blessed and she was seen.

"For it is with your heart that you believe and are justified, and it is with your mouth that you profess your faith and are saved" (Romans 10:10).

She can faintly hear people murmuring about her, something about a waste of money on the perfume, but she doesn't care. She thinks, "What is perfume when I have chosen to give Him my entire life. I have chosen to follow Him forever." In His perfect mercy, Jesus gave her new dignity as He defended her to the others.

"You did not give me any water for my feet, but she wet my feet with her tears and wiped them with her hair...she has poured perfume on my feet. Therefore, I tell you, her many sins have been forgiven - as her great love has shown." (portions of Luke 7:44, 46, 47)

"Why are you bothering this woman? She has done a beautiful thing to me. When she poured this perfume on my body, she did it to prepare me for burial. Truly I tell you,

> FOR IT IS WITH YOUR HEART THAT YOU BELIEVE AND ARE JUSTIFIED, AND IT IS WITH YOUR MOUTH THAT YOU PROFESS YOUR FAITH AND ARE SAVED.
>
> *Romans 10:10*

wherever this gospel is preached throughout the world, what she has done will also be told, in memory of her" (Matthew 10, 12-13).

It's not long after she anointed Him and prepared Him for burial that Jesus began preparing for His triumphal entry into Jerusalem. Palm Sunday's purpose in our lives is to prepare our hearts for Easter. As we humbly wave our palm branches, we wave our hearts. We simultaneously sing and bow our heads in recognition of Jesus as our King. In this moment we place Him in His rightful place in our lives, in the center and at the top. He is the boss of everything.

He is in charge of my life and decisions, and He is my leader. I gladly lay down my coat and bow to my humble King. I set down my ideas, plans and decisions, and I pick up a branch of praise to gladly wave it in expectation of all His goodness. Together let's wave our branches boldly and unabashed in front of the crowd to acknowledge Jesus and His highest place in our lives.

It's been several years since I was last in Israel and the Dominus Flevit Church. Though it has been years, I still need a humble Easter heart just like I prayed for that hot Mediterranean day. I need a heart that believes, that waves my palm branch boldy despite my circumstances, my fears and my anxieties. Just like He enveloped me in His presence as I kneeled in that tiny one room chapel shaped like a teardrop, I ask Him to wrap me in His presence as I navigate the chaos that surrounds me today.

It was my eleventh exam in less than three weeks, and I was still waiting for final results, decisions and treatment plans. I was completely humbled by the routine that had suddenly become my norm: a kind nurse walks in, hands me a pink gown and asks me to get undressed, over and over and over again. Each time I think to myself, "This can't be happening." Only days before I was celebrating birthdays, enjoying holiday dinners and shopping with my sweet family. I'm steeled in denial as I continue to think, "Surely it will all turn out to be nothing."

I'm escorted to a waiting area with six socially spaced chairs and six other women in pink gowns, all watching HGTV and silently waiting for our turns. As hard as it is to face what I'm facing, I'm jolted into the realization that they too are sitting here. I'm humbled at the thought of what news might be in store for them. My heart literally tightens, "Oh no." I look around the room, and my heart softens for these women. It's so pressing.

---

"WHEN HE SAW THE CROWDS, HE HAD COMPASSION ON THEM BECAUSE THEY WERE CONFUSED AND HELPLESS, LIKE SHEEP WITHOUT A SHEPHERD" (MATTHEW 9:36, NLT).

---

The interior design magic continues on, but I find it impossible to endure. I let my mind wander, and it drifts to Jesus. All of a sudden I feel the Lord with me, and I remember our conversations at the teardrop church on the Mount of Olives. All I can see is the backside of pink and pony tails, but that's more than enough for my heart to break. Silently, I begin to pray, "All the times I begged you to break my heart like yours, and now I'm sitting here thankful that I'm alive and that you placed your love inside of me. Lord, I never want to lose your compassion."

My mind is flooded with the hundreds of women I have sat with and witnessed God's arm wrap them in His compassionate presence over the years. Women in a Kenyan prison whom God mercifully saved, women in a tiny electrical church closet where we poured out our prayers, women throughout the City of Columbus that I've met, hugged, cried with and invited to join us in prayer, in worship and in His presence. "Thank you Lord. You have answered my prayers in Dominus Flevit years ago and now today. I literally cling to your compassionate heart, and to my believing heart, I clutch it like a diamond in my hand. I see them Lord. Here they are. I lift them before you now in prayer one by one. Please Lord, see me too."

Where do you find yourself today? Are you humbled by the circumstances that are out of your control? Are you weeping and broken for the sins of now and the sins of then? Are you like Mary, pouring out all you have in gratitude? Are you like the ones who place their coats on the dusty, rocky road and wave their branches in the air to welcome your King? Or maybe you are part of the crowd and this is all new to you, but you feel excitement welling up inside as you learn more and experience His presence for the first time. Wherever you are - weeping or worshipful, humbled or hiding, broken or bold, my prayer for you is that you would draw closer to Him as we walk through this holy season and reflect on the cross that Jesus faced for you and for me. I'm laying my pink robe at His feet.

> Will you let your heart be humbled, and allow your desperation for Him to draw you into His presence?

# LUKE 19:35-41

---

THEY BROUGHT IT TO JESUS, THREW THEIR CLOAKS ON THE COLT AND PUT JESUS ON IT. AS HE WENT ALONG, PEOPLE SPREAD THEIR CLOAKS ON THE ROAD. WHEN HE CAME NEAR THE PLACE WHERE THE ROAD GOES DOWN THE MOUNT OF OLIVES, THE WHOLE CROWD OF DISCIPLES BEGAN JOYFULLY TO PRAISE GOD IN LOUD VOICES FOR ALL THE MIRACLES THEY HAD SEEN: "BLESSED IS THE KING WHO COMES IN THE NAME OF THE LORD!" "PEACE IN HEAVEN AND GLORY IN THE HIGHEST!" SOME OF THE PHARISEES IN THE CROWD SAID TO JESUS, "TEACHER, REBUKE YOUR DISCIPLES!" "I TELL YOU," HE REPLIED, "IF THEY KEEP QUIET, THE STONES WILL CRY OUT." AS HE APPROACHED JERUSALEM AND SAW THE CITY, HE WEPT OVER IT AND SAID, "IF YOU, EVEN YOU, HAD ONLY KNOWN ON THIS DAY WHAT WOULD BRING YOU PEACE—BUT NOW IT IS HIDDEN FROM YOUR EYES."

# PRAYER

---

Father in heaven, I come before
you to lay down my coat. While I
am bowing low before you, I also
want to give you my past mistakes,
current sins and anything that is
holding me back from you. I lay it
all down before you. Now I take
up the palm branch of my heart
and wave a praise to you. I thank
you for loving me, praise you for
providing for me and worship you
for who you are to me. You are my
Savior, my king, my leader and my
first love. Amen.

*Pray this scripture over your own life:*
Lord, It is with my heart that I believe and am justified, and it is with my mouth that I profess my faith and am saved.

*For it is with your heart that you believe and are justified, and it is with your mouth that you profess your faith and are saved*

*Romans 10:10*

*words worth repeating*

JESUS, BOTH FULLY HUMAN AND FULLY DIVINE, WEPT.

WE NEED THE CROSS THAT YOU FACE.

I GLADLY LAY DOWN MY COAT AND BOW TO MY HUMBLE KING.

I CLING TO YOUR COMPASSIONATE HEART, AND I CLUTCH MY BELIEVING HEART LIKE A DIAMOND IN MY HAND.

# Reflect

WHETHER ON YOUR OWN OR IN A COMMUNITY OF OTHERS, ASK THESE QUESTIONS AND APPLY THEM TO YOUR LIFE.

# Read

JESUS' TRIUMPHAL ENTRY

Matthew 21:1-11
Mark 11:1-11
Luke 19:28-44
John 12:12-19

JESUS ANOINTED WITH PERFUME

Matthew 26:6-13
Mark 14:3-9
Luke 7:36-50
John 12:1-8

*Learn to weep for what causes Jesus to weep. What do you weep over? Take some time to weep before the Lord.*

*Learn humility by choosing to bow low through active prayer. Have I bowed in humility before Jesus recently? Kneel beside your bed tonight, and pray.*

*Give God your coat which represents the earthly treasure, identity, prestige or concern that consumes you. What "coats" do you need to lay down to make a path for Him?*

*What areas of your life still contain pride or an "I can do it myself" attitude? List, repent and release them to Him.*

*How can you symbolically wave a palm branch today? (Ideas: Pray aloud to acknowledge God's attributes. Read a Psalm out loud. Sing songs of praise.)*

*Prepare your heart for Easter. Prepare your heart to believe. How much time will you spend with God each day between now and Easter?*

*Who are you in the crowd? The faithful? The hopeful? The doubting? The wondering? Who do you want to be?*

SPRING EASTER MENU

Every good meal needs a centerpiece and beef
tenderloin is certainly delicious. If you prefer ham,
I think a Honey Baked ham from the store is easiest
and best. Here is our Easter menu. I will include all
of these recipes, one at the end of each chapter.

## Appetizer

MOM'S DEVILED EGGS

## Main Dish

UNCLE ALLEN'S
BEEF TENDERLOIN

## Salad

RACHEL PATTON'S
SPRING PEAR SALAD

## Side

ELAINE BARTEL'S
EASY CHEESY POTATOES

## Bread

GRANDMOTHER JACKSON'S
BRAIDED PIMENTO CHEESE BREAD

## Dessert

COCONUT CAKE

## MOM'S DEVILED EGGS

My mom is an incredible seamstress. She even made my wedding gown. Easter was a holiday she intended to always make special. One year she designed pastel Easter dresses for me and my sister. Mom always had a gallon of good Southern sweet tea in the fridge after church and of course these yummy deviled eggs! Here's a note from my Mom, who lives with a gracious and loving Easter heart.

# DIRECTIONS

Hi Jen, Until today, I have never measured the ingredients that I use for deviled eggs, but this time I wrote down the amount that I used for each ingredient.

First, I boiled 8 large white eggs. After cooling them in ice water, I halved them and removed the yolks.

I mashed all the ingredients together with a fork. Then I filled each egg half with about a tablespoon of the filling. I lightly sprinkled the tops with paprika. I usually leave a few without paprika in case some people (especially children) don't like it.

*Make 16 deviled eggs*

Enjoy!
Love, Mom

# INGREDIENTS

8 egg yolks, mashed
¼ cup finely diced dill pickles
*(I normally use hamburger dill pickle slices)*
2 Tbs. dill pickle juice
¼ cup mayonnaise
1 tsp. yellow mustard

The amount of pickles, juice, mayo, and mustard can be adjusted to suit your taste.

*Dominus Flevit Church (center right)*

*Dominus Flevit Church*

*Inside Dominus Flevit Church*

*Doyle and Jennifer at Beit She'an, one of the oldest cities in Istreal.*

*The view out a window of the school we attended in Jerusalem*

*Jesus, I am desperate
for you, your will
and your presence.*

# The Garden

## A DESPERATE HEART

I'm definitely not in a garden. I don't even have a view of trees outside my apartment window. All I can see are the windows and white doors of other apartments. Hopefully one day we will move to the countryside again, where my heart is the fullest, where the hills roll and the birds sing, but for now I see only white.

I love to rise at 4 a.m. when everything is quiet. I sit with my Bible and pray to God. He talks to me, not audibly, but in my heart – my believing Easter heart, and He talks to me through His love letters to me. I read them over and over; I never tire of His word.

On this particular morning, it is still dark outside, and my mind whirls with the report from yesterday. "Yes, Jennifer, you did test positive for breast cancer," the surgeon says on the phone. Only God can undo this. Only He can walk me through this. I cry out to Him. Sitting in my all white garden, I'm all alone.

AT LEAST THERE IS HOPE FOR A TREE: IF IT IS CUT DOWN, IT WILL SPROUT AGAIN, AND ITS NEW SHOOTS WILL NOT FAIL.

*Job 14:7*

Gethsemane means "oil press," a place of pressing, and because of Gethsemane's role in Jesus' story, the word also means a place of suffering and agony. It was there on the Mount of Olives in the Garden of Gethsemane, the evening before His crucifixion, that Jesus gathered his best friends to pray. He faced the cross, and He faced it alone. There are some things in this life that, even when we are surrounded by friends or family, we still have to walk the steps alone. For Jesus, that was the cross. No one else could complete that task of love but Him. So He prayed.

*He prayed to the Father in agony of soul - is there any other way?*

"And being in anguish, he prayed more earnestly, and his sweat was like drops of blood falling to the ground" (Luke 22:44).

Jesus begged and cried and pleaded with the Father. In His humanity, Jesus likely wondered, "Can we try something different? Maybe there is another or better plan." He kept checking on his friends to see if they were awake and praying, but instead they had fallen asleep. If only they would awaken and join Jesus, maybe then God would do something. Maybe then God would change His mind. But God didn't. The plan was Jesus and the cross. Agony and death.

"Jesus finally conceded, 'Father, if You are willing, take this cup from Me. Yet not My will, but Yours be done'" (Luke 22:42).

At the cross our will and God's will cross. At the cross we nail down our ways, our plans and even our ideas of how we think things should be. I don't know about you, but I have a very strong will. I like having things my way - a lot. Before we go to the cross, we lay down our coats and we say, "Your will be done in my life, Lord Jesus."

I don't want to have cancer. I don't want that word and my name anywhere near each other. But no matter how hard I will it, I cannot change my circumstances. And so I give it all to Jesus. I nail it all to His cross.

*And so I give it all to Jesus.*
*I nail it all to His cross.*

What are you facing today in your garden? Do you feel as if friends or family are sleeping while you are desperately praying? Not only does Jesus want to share in our suffering, He DOES share in our suffering. He truly understands.

Despite everything that Jesus knew He would soon face and despite the very tough road ahead, Jesus prayed for you and for me. In His anguish and desperation, He prayed for us. Isn't that incredible?

"Holy Father, protect them by the power of your name, the name you gave me, so that they may be one as we are one. . . My prayer is not that you take them out of the world but that you protect them from the evil one. They are not of the world, even as I am not of it. Sanctify them by the truth; your

word is truth. . . I have given them the glory that you gave me, that they may be one as we are one - I in them and you in me - so that they may be brought to complete unity. Then the world will know that you sent me and have loved them even as you have loved me"
(John 17:11, 15-17, 22-23).

There it is! In red letters, there is the prayer straight from Jesus Himself for us!

*He prayed for you and for me to believe, To have a believing heart. That is Easter.*

Hiking in the heat of Israel, especially around Jerusalem, is literally my favorite thing to do. Doyle and I never ever tire of it. We go everywhere until our feet throb and legs ache, and then we sit and relish our experiences at a coffee cafe on Ben Yehuda Street or at an Armenian pizza shop in the Old City. I have dozens of memories like that, yet one is most prominent.

It started with a hike to the Garden of Gethsemane where we stopped along the dusty, rocky paths lined with vibrant green and blooms to marvel at the magnificence of the ancient olive trees. Thousands of years old, they are huge with gnarled branches from grafting after grafting. I'm amazed that even in these old gnarled trees, God had a message for early believers. In their judgements of each other, God reminded them that His grace and mercy extends to both the Jew and the Gentile. The gnarled trees remind me that God has shown me such grace and mercy, and no matter the offense, no one is so broken that they cannot be grafted into God's family tree.

"And don't get to feeling superior to those pruned branches down on the ground. If they don't persist in remaining deadwood, they could very well get grafted back in. God can do that. He can perform miracle grafts. Why, if he could graft you—branches cut from a tree out in the wild—into an orchard tree, he certainly isn't going to have any trouble grafting branches back into the tree they grew from in the first place. Just be glad you're in the tree, and hope for the best for the others" (Romans 11:24, The Message).

From the garden, we hiked back down the mountain and around toward the new city of Jerusalem. Ice cream sounded really good in the heat, and they have the best in the world at Caravel. Our budget was beyond tight as a young married couple, but we always had ice cream money for our hikes. I was already dreaming about my very own large chocolate swirl which is huge, or "gadol" as they say in Hebrew.

Ben Yahuda Street is a beauty with fresh flowers in buckets, fun paper stationery shops, cute cafes and a slow pace. I love exquisite pens and pretty paper, and I was mesmerized by the charm that surrounded me along our way. As we walked, I said to Doyle, "Let's take a break and listen to this man playing the violin." String instruments are my favorite, and so we sat and listened to the violinist for a while.

As the lovely music filled my ears, a quick thought tugged on my heart, "Give him the ice cream money." I paused, still dreaming about my gadol chocolate, a soon-to-be refreshing treat on an increasingly hot day. The tug deepened. My mouth watering, I considered the long, hot walk back home and my desire to cool off with a deliciously cold treat. Before I even realized what I was saying, I turned to Doyle, "Honey, is it okay if today we give him our ice cream money?"

Kindly Doyle replied, "You don't even know him. Are you sure?"

"Yes, I feel it strongly, that we need to give him the money."

Willing to oblige, Doyle and I both emptied our pockets, placed our money in the bucket and began the two mile walk back to our adorable little apartment in the Old City. Even in the heat and even without the ice cream, I felt a refreshing joy that lightened my steps. I thought, "Who cares about ice cream today. Obedience feels better than sacrifice."

---

BUT SAMUEL REPLIED: "DOES THE LORD DELIGHT IN BURNT OFFERINGS AND SACRIFICES AS MUCH AS IN OBEYING THE LORD? TO OBEY IS BETTER THAN SACRIFICE, AND TO HEED IS BETTER THAN THE FAT OF RAMS." *1 Samuel 15:22*

---

The next morning I woke early, and I found myself making sandwiches and packing fruit. I was going back to find the musician; he needed a good lunch! I added a fresh cucumber salad to the packed lunch and headed out to find him. Sure enough, he was exactly where we left him the day before. My heart was drawn toward him, and he met me with visible gratitude. I discovered that he was a new immigrant and only spoke Russian. Despite the language barrier, a routine began that included daily check-ins, packed lunches, ice cream money and prayer.

---

GOD HAD CONNECTED US, AND IN
A STORY THAT ONLY GOD COULD
WRITE, WE BECAME FRIENDS WITH THE
RUSSIAN VIOLINIST.

---

One day I grabbed the Jerusalem Post and ran to Doyle saying, "Look, he's on the front page! I just knew it. I just knew that He was a good guy. I just knew that God put that man on our hearts for a reason!" On the front page of the local newspaper was a picture of the Russian violinist. They explained that he had been famous in Russia but finally made "Aliya." Aliya is the immigration of Jews to Israel from the land where they had been displaced. Now home in Israel, he was caring for his blind mother. I prayed, "Lord, thank you for this sweet family; provide for all their needs. I'm touched that you would show me the truth of their story. Help me to see their desperate hearts, to have compassion and respond. Give me more opportunities to love them, and open my eyes. Amen."

Just down the road from the Garden of Gethsemane, God invited me into a new story. I didn't know the desperation that the man from Russia had endured. I didn't know the life he had been living before arriving home to Israel. But God knew. He knew, and through His prompting, I was invited to be a conduit of God's love, compassion, grace and mercy amidst this man's desperation.

When Jesus faced His final earthly hours, He invited His disciples into the garden and a much greater story. But in their humanity, the disciples fell short. When asked to pray, they slept. I just can't stay mad at the disciples for too long, can you? At first I thought, *Really? You really can't pray with Jesus for one single hour? That is ridiculous! He told you what He was facing. He warned you that the future of the entire world was at stake, and you guys slept right through it. What kind of friends are you?* Lame, lame, lame! Then I began to see myself in them. How many times have I chosen my own creature comforts over spending time with the Lord? How many times have I hoarded my ice cream money despite God's invitation to give? "God, forgive me. I do want more of You, and I do believe. Help me to change."

Scripture tells us that as Jesus confronted His sleeping disciples, a crowd arrived to seize Him. Jesus went from the crushing betrayal of His friends sleeping through the toughest spiritual moments He had ever faced to the meanest group of betrayers arriving to physically attack Him. Can you imagine that whirlwind? He was bombarded on all sides mentally, emotionally, spiritually and physically.

As the men arrived with clubs and swords prepared for a violent entrance into the peaceful garden, they asked for Jesus. *Where is Jesus?* Jesus responded with the most incredible three words of power: "I AM He."

*With three small words, the men fell to the ground.*

"Jesus, knowing all that was going to happen to him, went out and asked them, 'Who is it you want?' 'Jesus of Nazareth,' they replied. 'I am he,' Jesus said. (And Judas the traitor was standing there with them.) When Jesus said, 'I am he,' they drew back and fell to the ground" (John 18:4-6).

His enemies were in the dust and down for the count! In those three words Jesus reflected back to the Old Testament and declared to the world that He was there in power at the beginning, and He will be with us in power until the end of time.

By that point in the garden, sleeping Peter, now awake, was full of energy, and he jumped forward in defense of His Savior King. With a fire in his belly and a sword in his hand, Peter was ready to fight. In one fell swoop, Peter cut off an ear of one of the soldiers.

Pause a moment here; I just love this! I know, I know, we shouldn't be cheering on this type of behavior, but YES, I feel it! I feel Peter's passion for protection of the One he loved. That same fire, energy and spirit fill me up when I think of my beloved Savior, and so I declare, "Lord, may I always boldly defend you too. I never want my fire to slow. I love you, and I believe in you."

True to His healing character, Jesus bent down and picked up the ear and placed it back on the man's head. Healing in the midst of chaos, that's Jesus! He offered a

WHEN JESUS SAID, 'I AM HE,' THEY DREW BACK AND FELL TO THE GROUND.

*John 18:6*

miracle in the middle of a battle. There are healings and miracles waiting for you too, right now in the center of the struggles that you face.

The captors came and asked, "Where is the Christ?" Jesus stepped up, and He said to them, "I AM HE." At the sound of His voice they fell to the ground. His enemies literally fell and hit the ground. They came with swords, but Jesus met them in peace and confidence. They arrived with weapons for battle, but Jesus acted in humility and healing. My prayer for you right now is that you will leave your enemies on the ground just as Jesus did. I want you to receive the peace and confidence that is available to you because of His name and authority. Jesus' enemies fell straight down at the sound of His voice, and our enemies have to bow to Him as well. This is the mighty power of the name of Jesus. His healing and power are greater than any diagnosis, any fear or any foe. **I AM HE**.

Maybe you are thinking, what enemies? Maybe you aren't facing physical persecution yet, verbal backlash or violent threats because of your faith. Maybe you are relatively well-liked, and you live a life void of much conflict. Though Jesus faced physical enemies in the Garden of Gethsemane, He also faced spiritual

THERE ARE HEALINGS AND MIRACLES WAITING FOR YOU TOO, RIGHT NOW IN THE CENTER OF THE STRUGGLES THAT YOU FACE.

enemies, and so do we. We also endure unseen attacks on our spirit by our enemies. Have you ever suffered ongoing discouragement? Have you ever believed a lie about yourself, your skin color, your accent or your personality that was contrary to the truths of God's word? Have you ever felt a gloomy malaise over your day or your week, a grey fog that you just couldn't shake? Those were likely the works of an unseen spiritual enemy.

Three words from Jesus, I AM HE, and those enemies must flee. One breath from the mouth of God, the great I AM, and our enemies must fall to the ground. That is the mighty power of our Savior and God.

*Our enemies are laughably weak against the almighty power of Jesus.*

I encourage you to identify any enemy that is holding you back from God's very best for your life. Leave that lie, attack or plot of the enemy, and leave it right here, right now. Leave it at the feet of Jesus who says to our enemies, I AM HE!

Following His arrest, Jesus headed toward the cross. The closer Jesus got to His final hour, the greater the torment, desperation and betrayal that confronted Him. Peter denied Him three times. Judas double-crossed Him with a betrayer's kiss. Again and again, Jesus suffered. No matter what we face - no matter the hurt, the pain or the agony, Jesus understands.

We often think of a garden as a beautiful place, and the Garden of Gethsemane truly is beautiful. But the truest beauty of that place comes from the pain that Jesus endured there. In that garden, east of Jerusalem near the foot of the Mount of Olives, Jesus faced great agony, betrayal and desperation. And in that place, God met Jesus. In that agony, God showed up. In that desperation, God was there.

I'm reminded of God's beautiful presence as I sit in my garden of all white, struggling through these medical reports. My all white garden is quiet, and I'm desperate for the Lord. But even in this place of sadness and fear, I have an overwhelming sense that God is with me, and it's beautiful.

No matter how desolate, no matter how broken, no matter how dark and no matter how lonely, it is never hopeless because there is always Jesus.

*And where there is Jesus, there is hope.*

In the short time that I've been on this unwanted medical journey, I have been desperate. I am desperate for the circumstances to change, the results to be different and the journey to be easier. I am desperate for a miracle, and I am desperately faithful that God will bring healing. I am desperate in this garden. But the most beautiful thing has happened because of my desperation. God has shown up and met me in my desperation. When I was hungry, He fed me the bread of life. When I was thirsty, He gave me living water. When I was cold, He blanketed me in His comfort.

When I was tear-stained, He wept with me and held me close.

HIS GOODNESS HAS BEEN EVER PRESENT THROUGHOUT EVERY STEP OF MY DESPERATION.

I imagine that Jesus knew this comfort too. Not only that, but Jesus understood His place in creation. Jesus understood that the plan for redemption involved Him and the cross, agony and death. I too understand that my journey has purpose. Though I don't always understand God's ways, I do understand that there is so much more to this story that I cannot see. Jesus was a part of something bigger, and so am I. Even in my most difficult days, I am called to share my hope, and my hope is Jesus.

As I sit in my garden, I wonder, did Jesus pray to be miraculously delivered from the circumstances around Him? I think about the many people I have seen healed by the miraculous hand of God. I believe in that healing. I pray for that healing. And I also pray that no matter how God brings healing into my life, He will give me exactly what I need to get through it. He will remain with me, and He will remain my hope.

EVEN IN MY MOST DIFFICULT DAYS, I AM CALLED TO SHARE MY HOPE, AND MY HOPE IS JESUS.

Do you know that kind of a garden? A place that is gnarled and full of blood, sweat and tears. A place that is both dusty, rocky paths and vibrant green and blooms. A place where God meets you in your disappointment, sadness and desperation, and in the presence of God, you discover exquisite beauty. A place where there is Jesus and there is hope.

## IN THE GARDEN
*Hymn by C. Austin Miles*

I come to the garden alone,
While the dew is still on the roses,
And the voice I hear falling on my ear,
The Son of God discloses.

And He walks with me, and He talks with me,
And He tells me I am His own,
And the joy we share as we tarry there,
None other has ever known.

He speaks, and the sound of His voice
Is so sweet the birds hush their singing;
And the melody that He gave to me
Within my heart is ringing.
I'd stay in the garden with Him
Tho' the night around me be falling;
But He bids me go; thro' the voice of woe,
His voice to me is calling.

How have you suffered, and in your desperation, have you discovered Jesus and His perfect comfort, peace and love?

# LUKE 22:39-46

———————

JESUS WENT OUT AS USUAL TO THE MOUNT OF OLIVES, AND HIS DISCIPLES FOLLOWED HIM. ON REACHING THE PLACE, HE SAID TO THEM, "PRAY THAT YOU WILL NOT FALL INTO TEMPTATION." HE WITHDREW ABOUT A STONE'S THROW BEYOND THEM, KNELT DOWN AND PRAYED, "FATHER, IF YOU ARE WILLING, TAKE THIS CUP FROM ME; YET NOT MY WILL, BUT YOURS BE DONE." AN ANGEL FROM HEAVEN APPEARED TO HIM AND STRENGTHENED HIM. AND BEING IN ANGUISH, HE PRAYED MORE EARNESTLY, AND HIS SWEAT WAS LIKE DROPS OF BLOOD FALLING TO THE GROUND.

WHEN HE ROSE FROM PRAYER AND WENT BACK TO THE DISCIPLES, HE FOUND THEM ASLEEP, EXHAUSTED FROM SORROW. "WHY ARE YOU SLEEPING?" HE ASKED THEM. "GET UP AND PRAY SO THAT YOU WILL NOT FALL INTO TEMPTATION."

# PRAYER

---

Jesus, I'm desperate for you.
I'm facing a battle that is
too much. These are not the
circumstances that I would
choose. Help me to find you
in my sadness, disappointment
and desperation. Help me to
be a person who finds the
beauty along the dusty, rocky
paths. I want your will for my
life, and I need your strength
to carry me. Amen.

*Pray this scripture
over your own life:*
Jesus, by the power
of your name, my
enemies must fall to
the ground and flee.
Thank you for your
almighty power.

*When Jesus said,
'I am he,' they
drew back and fell
to the ground.*

John 18:6

## words worth repeating

GETHSEMANE MEANS "OIL PRESS," A
PLACE OF PRESSING.

AT THE CROSS OUR WILL AND GOD'S
WILL CROSS.

IN HIS ANGUISH AND DESPERATION,
JESUS PRAYED FOR ME.

NO ONE IS SO BROKEN THAT THEY
CANNOT BE GRAFTED INTO GOD'S
FAMILY TREE.

OBEDIENCE FEELS BETTER THAN
SACRIFICE.

HEALINGS AND MIRACLES ARE WAITING
FOR ME AMIDST MY STRUGGLES.

ONE WORD FROM JESUS, I AM HE, AND
MY ENEMIES MUST FLEE.

# Reflect

WHETHER ON YOUR OWN OR IN A COMMUNITY OF OTHERS, ASK THESE QUESTIONS AND APPLY THEM TO YOUR LIFE.

# Read

JESUS IN THE GARDEN OF GETHSEMANE

Matthew 26: 36-56

Mark 14: 32-52

Luke 22: 39-53

John 18: 1-14

*You are invited to be a part of a God's story. What does it look like for you to be part of God's story?*

*What have you done as an act of passion for Jesus? How might your life be different if you lived with a fire in your belly for Jesus?*

*What in your life feels pressing, like olives in an oil press? In your desperation, Jesus is there. Where there is Jesus, there is hope.*

*Nail your ways, plans and ideas to the cross. Lay them down, and pray God's will for your life.*

*List the enemies that you are facing. Remember the power available to you. In the name of Jesus, your enemies must flee. What lie, attack or plot of the enemy do you need to leave behind?*

*How have you seen God heal you or a loved one? What miracle are you praying for today?*

## BEEF TENDERLOIN
*With Horseradish Sauce*

Pastor Allen Jackson is my wonderful brother-n-love of almost 30 years. He has an unwavering Easter heart, and he shares that belief with me and the thousands of people he has encountered throughout his life. The many family meals centered around Jesus and Allen's tenderloin have been a joy and a strength for me throughout the decades that we've been family.

When my boys were teenagers, they wanted hearty food, so I learned how to make Pastor Allen's beef tenderloin. I admit, his is better than mine (he uses a smoker and some liquid smoke while I cook mine in the oven). Nevertheless, my guys often said, "Mom, can we make Uncle Allen's steak for dinner tonight?"

Do your best with whatever you have on hand. Recipes are to be passed along as reminders of adored family members.

For a large crowd, I buy my beef tenderloin trimmed from Sam's Club. For a smaller group, I cut and freeze half. I take a sharp knife and remove any and all fat (unless your butcher will do that for you.)

## DIRECTIONS

Get your tenderloin to room temperature by rubbing it down on both sides with vegetable or canola oil. Then deeply rub in a good steak seasoning or simply use salt, pepper and garlic powder. I like lots of spice. Have fun with it.

Preheat your oven to 425 while you get out your largest iron skillet (a Dutch oven works fine).

### Cooking Guide

| | |
|---|---|
| **RARE** | 115°F – 120°F |
| **MEDIUM RARE** | 120°F – 125°F |
| **MEDIUM** | 130°F – 135°F |

In the skillet, I add another tablespoon of oil and get the skillet hot. Then I place the meat in the skillet to sear for 3-5 minutes on each side. Once the meat is seared, place it in a hot oven for 20-25 minutes. Let it rest for 15 minutes to keep the juices inside before cutting.

Keep in mind that the internal temperature will continue to rise about 5 to 7 degrees after being removed from the oven.

## HORSERADISH SAUCE

Fresh horseradish can be found in the seafood section of your grocery store. Mix as much as you like with sour cream. I find that 3-4 table-spoons to 1 cup is a perfect ratio for most people.

## BLUE CHEESE SAUCE

½ Blue cheese crumble container with 1-2 cups sour cream. Again this is to your taste and number of guests. I use half the container of cheese, and mix it with my mixer until the blue cheese is whipped into the sour cream.

*Garden of Gethsemane*

*Jennifer in front of the Mount of Olives*

*Jennifer on Ben Yehuda Street 1992*

*Jennifer in an olive grove in Isreal*

*Olive trees in the Garden of Gethsemane*

---

*Lord, I pick up my
cross and follow you.*

# The Cross

## A SUFFERING HEART

The world is whirling around me. I shift from numb to shock to, "It will be okay." The harsh reality is sinking in. Multiple doctors confirm that I have breast cancer. "God is so much bigger, Jennifer," I say out loud as I drive downtown to the hospital for my appointment.

Because of the pandemic, no visitors are allowed with me, so I make my way through traffic and parking all alone. Through my windshield, the city skyline rises with the sun, and I pray, "God, thank you for beautiful Columbus. I love our city, and I know you do too. Bring peace, salvation and revival to many across this beautiful, expansive city. And Lord, I also need peace. I need courage for this test today. I'm by myself, and I've never been through anything like this. Though I have walked alongside many others through times like this, today is my first time facing a trial like this one."

> I HAVE COME THAT THEY MAY HAVE LIFE, AND HAVE IT TO THE FULL.
>
> *John 10:10b*

Though I face the steps of my path alone, I know that God is with me. I continue to pray, whispering my memory verse to God and to my heart,

---

WHEN HARD PRESSED, I CRIED TO THE LORD; HE BROUGHT ME INTO A SPACIOUS PLACE. THE LORD IS WITH ME; I WILL NOT BE AFRAID. WHAT CAN MERE MORTALS DO TO ME?

*Psalm 118:5-6*

---

A bit like a scatterbrained zombie walking under all the strain and stress of this new medical path, I realize I'm at the wrong building. The lady at the counter instructs me, "Ma'am, you need to cross the street, go through those double doors, up the stairs and around to your left." As I pull my coat back on and prepare to cross the street on a cold January morning, I start to giggle as I think, "This mice maze is kind of funny, and don't worry, Jennifer, you will make it in plenty of time."

I finally make it to the correct building and the correct check-in table. There is a kind, gentle lady who greets me and hands me paperwork. She says, "I will need to take your picture for identity." As she looks down at my name on the form, she says, "Oh, you are Jennifer Jackson?"

"Yes ma'am."

In the most complimentary way, she says, "Well honey, I have been following your church online, so tell that sweet pastor husband of yours that we just love him so much!"

My heart filled with hope. "Thank you, we have been praying for this city and its people."

"Well sweet girl, I will be praying for you."

I could feel her kindness, and it filled my heart. My Easter believing heart was in there and beating loudly now. But nothing could be as loud as the sound of the MRI machine. Whew! They don't prepare you for that. Tap, tap tap, bing, bing bing. Were they jack hammering? What are they doing? In between scans and noises I hear my music selection shouting through. It's Lauren Daigle singing, "I know you're trying hard to just be strong, And it's a fight just to keep it together, together. Just take one step closer. Put one foot in front of the other. You'll get through this. Just follow the light in the darkness. You're gonna be okay."

THOUGH IT SOUNDS LIKE I'M IN THE MIDDLE OF A MAJOR CONSTRUCTION ZONE, I CAN STILL FEEL GOD'S PRESENCE RIGHT BY MY SIDE. NO MATTER WHAT SURROUNDS ME, GOD IS WITH ME.

Eventually the machine and the noises stop. The test is finally over, thank the Lord. With the lights back on, I see jagged lines across my field of vision. The nurse tells me that it's a side effect of the lights and sounds, and I'm experiencing a normal post-MRI headache. After I check out, walk through the hallway, back down the stairs, out the garage and start my drive home, my new reality begins to set in.

I pick up the phone and call my sister. She is often the

one I call when I need support, encouragement or therapeutic laughter. I give her a brief update, sharing with her the unexpected moments of this new journey. I found out that because of the biopsy, I'm less able to do things that require me to lift my arms over my head. If or when I have surgery, I will need physical therapy to get back my full range of motion in my arms. I jokingly confess to my sister, "Brenna, I think the worst part of all this is that I won't be able to get my Spanx over my head!" Our together laughter gives me hope.

Sisters are special aren't they? I'm so grateful for the sisters, biological and spiritual, in my life. I'm so grateful for the women in my life. The women in my life have breathed courage into some of my toughest moments. Laughter, friendship and words of truth - all of it has given me courage when I needed it.

The women at the base of the cross remind me of the women in my life. Don't you just love the women at the base of the cross? Scripture tells us that many women were there, watching from a distance (Matthew 27:55). "Among them were Mary Magdalene, Mary the mother of James and Joseph, and the mother of Zebedee's sons" (Matthew

LAUGHTER, FRIENDSHIP AND WORDS OF TRUTH - ALL OF IT HAS GIVEN ME COURAGE WHEN I NEEDED IT.

27:56). John 19:25 tells us that, "Near the cross of Jesus stood his mother, his mother's sister, Mary the wife of Clopas, and Mary Magdalene."

I think about these gals and how they were just ordinary women like you and like me. I love how they are identified as moms, sisters and wives. I am all of those, and so I relate to these women. It just feels so normal to read about them.

---

THEY WERE LIVING ORDINARY LIVES WITH ORDINARY DUTIES AND AN ORDINARY LOVE FOR AN EXTRAORDINARY SAVIOR.

---

From the moment the word on the street made it to these gals - word that Jesus was with Pilot - I imagine that they rallied tightly together. They were there from the moment Jesus began His cross-filled walk to Golgotha, and they found a way to squeeze through the crowds and keep up pace with Him. In and out of faces who were just there to gawk and gossip, they pushed through the people, mothering Jesus from the sidelines by keeping at least one eye on Him at all times. As they stayed right with Him every step of the way, I imagine they were prayerful and tearful, witnessing His pain and wondering about what He would soon endure.

These were brave women. It could not have been easy to remain so emotionally and physically devoted to Jesus in His final days, but they stuck to Him like a warrior army - committed, protective and fierce. Their courage gives me courage. With so much unknown ahead of me, I want to be devoted to Jesus like these women were devoted to Jesus. I want to be committed, protective and fierce. Their example encourages me. What about you? Are you facing something in your life where you need courage?

"In Galilee these women had followed him and cared for his needs. Many other women who had come up with him to Jerusalem were also there" (Mark 15:41).

Mary knew that she had the best friends in the world. They stuck to her like glue even under the realization that this mob was dangerous and they should probably be at home with the kids. But instead they would go all the way to the cross. This army of women was Mary's support team. Nothing was beyond their commitment to each other and their commitment to Jesus.

*No matter how hard it got.
They were all in.*

And it got hard. Jesus could barely keep going as He carried the weight of the cross on His back. Matthew tells us that the soldiers spit on Jesus, and then they struck him over and over on the head with a staff (Matthew 27:30). Beaten, tired, sweating and bleeding, Jesus continued. Luke tells us that the women mourned and wailed for Him (Luke 23:27).

Scripture tells us that another man began to carry the cross for Jesus, a tiny ray of hope and momentary relief for our desperate Savior. I imagine the women, still keeping up, and crying out as they followed Jesus. I imagine their thoughts and conversations along the way and later when they recalled what they had witnessed. "Can you believe the people spitting and rejecting Him? Just last week they were listening to Him teach us. How can they be so two faced? He must be so embarrassed that they would take His clothes and mock Him with a fake crown. The emotional cruelty is unbearable. He never hurt any of them; He showed only love."

His head down, His blood dripping and His strength weakening, His body likely went into shock. Mary and John, experiencing their own shock, held hands and stayed together as they swerved in and out of the obnoxious crowd.

Jesus' friends huddled together and watched the most traumatic event of His life and their own lives unfold. They maintained their commitment to Jesus as He breathed His last breath, and they maintained their commitment to Jesus' mother, Mary, as her heart broke. Sometimes it's good when friends just sit with you in the hard, and so there they sat at the foot of the cross together.

> THEY SHARED JESUS.
> THEY SERVED JESUS.
> THEY FED JESUS.
> THEY OBEYED JESUS.
> THEY FOLLOWED JESUS.
> THEY RALLIED FOR JESUS.
> THEY PREPARED HIS BODY.
> THEY ANOINTED HIS FEET.
> THEY NEVER LEFT HIS PIERCED SIDE.

Jesus exhausted everything hard on the cross that we might experience everything good from Him.

I was experiencing much of the good that Jesus provided for me on the cross as a totally in love newlywed. I was living in awe that I got to marry my dream guy and that we were setting out together on a journey to serve Jesus for the rest of our lives in ministry. We were in Israel, attending school and studying the Bible, and it was the highlight of my life. Despite all we learned, I felt most overwhelmed when I thought about the cross and the enormously hard sacrifices Jesus made for me and for all of us. "I'm unworthy Lord, You alone have the power and strength that I'm going to need to prepare myself as a pastor's wife. I am woefully inadequate but willing to learn and grow. Teach me everything I need to know. Amen." That was the cry of my heart.

AS A SOUTHERN GIRL AT HEART, I STILL FIXED MY HAIR, PUT ON A TOUCH OF MAKEUP AND DONNED CUTE TENNIS SHOES EVEN FOR HIKING CLASS.

I was determined to soak in every Bible verse, look at every rock in all of Israel and put my heart into understanding the history, geography and archaeology of everything, all while having fun with my cute, new husband. One of the classes we took was called Hiking Through the Physical Settings of the Bible. Israel is chock-full of historical and archaeological evidence of the cross, and so much of learning that history and archaeology comes through walking the land. Hiking classes always felt like a date to me. A Southern girl at heart, I still fixed my hair, put on a touch of makeup and donned cute tennis shoes even for hiking class.

It was going to be a long day of walking through the Old City with our New Testament professor, Bill Shlagel, and Gabriel Barkai, a world famous Archaeologist of the Old City. Professor Barkai taught us to look for God in the details, in the Bible and on the ground. As we were walking, he bent down and picked up a widow's mite coin from the road, "See, it's the little things that mean so much in archaeology." We continued our hike, pausing at each station of the cross for greater instruction. Each station represented a different stop on Jesus' path toward His crucifixion.

---

I FELT A MIX OF EXCITEMENT AND
HEARTACHE AS I IMAGINED WHAT IT
MUST HAVE BEEN LIKE FOR JESUS TO
ENDURE SUCH A SACRIFICE FOR US.

---

Our walk began on a street called the Via Delarosa. I was energized by the sights and sounds that surrounded us, including the cute, smoke grey donkeys loaded down with carts and blankets. I wondered if they were the same size as the donkey that Jesus rode on Palm Sunday. It's fascinating to me that over 2,000 years later there are still donkeys in Israel, and I'm reminded of Jesus' humility as I see firsthand the simplicity and stature of the cute donkeys.

As we walked along the crowded streets and paused to wait our turn at the next station on our route, I was distracted by the shops that lined the Jerusalem streets. Inside one shop I saw mounds of exotic spices including one with a small tag that said Frankincense. Once again I was struck that here they sold the same spice that the wise men brought to Bethlehem to welcome a baby, a baby who was born to die. Snapping out of my daydream, I heard our professor, "We have arrived at the first station, the station where Pilot condemned Jesus to die."

Deep in thought as we walked up hill after hill, our teacher read the scriptures of Jesus bearing the wood, the crown, the robe, the lashes, ultimately the nails and finally the cross. Jesus suffered each moment of the procession so that you and I might have life.

---

JESUS SUFFERED EACH
MOMENT OF THE
PROCESSION SO THAT YOU
AND I MIGHT HAVE LIFE.

---

ON THE
CROSS JESUS
ENDURED
SO MANY
CRUSHING
WOUNDS.

On the cross Jesus endured so many crushing wounds. He endured every punishment that you and I deserve. He literally placed our sins on His back, our curses on His head and our poverty and shame on His nakedness. He was rejected, nailed and hung. He was crucified. He did all of that in willing obedience to the Father, and He did all of that for you and for me.

Why? Why would someone do that? He came and lived and died for so many reasons. He wanted to offer us a solution to the evil we face and the sin in which we participate.

He came that we might have life and have it abundantly (John 10:10). He wants us to live this abundant life here on earth but also to live with Him in eternity forever. He covered everything on the cross. He didn't forget something we need, and He didn't leave anything out. He gave us access to His blessings, wholeness, acceptance, forgiveness, healing and a right relationship with God.

*He came that we might have life and have it abundantly.*

Jesus became our salvation. This historic event of crucifixion provided everything for us. On the cross He conquered death and evil. Are you willing to leave your sin on the cross with Him? To truly put it behind you once and for all? He provided forgiveness for anything we have done in the past and anything we will do in the future (and that passing sinful thought you just had - yep, He covers that too). I know, the grace offered is overwhelmingly good, but take it! This is the gift of the cross!

# SIMPLY CROSS

at the cross we simply cross over
WE CROSS
from dark to light
from despair to hope
from sick to whole
WE CROSS
from prison to free
from broken to repaired
from shamed to accepted
WE CROSS
from need to provision
from bitter to forgiven
from hell to heaven
at the foot of the cross
WE CROSS
from impossible to miraculous
SIMPLY CROSS OVER

~ *Jennifer Jackson*

It never ceases to amaze me that on the cross God covered everything we need here on earth in addition to giving us the promise of a future home in heaven. The cross offers us such gracious love and mighty power, all in such a personal way. The healing, acceptance, provision and forgiveness is specific to our needs, our emptiness and our sins.

*We are forgiven because He died in our place.*

We are forgiven because He died in our place. He offers us deliverance from our sin. On the cross, one single event made so much available to us. We have access to healing, peace, joy, health, heaven, provision and so much more. Understanding what the cross has to offer gives us permanent stability and confidence that cannot be shaken.

Because of everything He suffered, He understands hardships, pain and suffering beyond anyone else in my life. Even as I endure appointments, tests, bad news, disappointments, another waiting room and another thin, pink gown, my suffering Savior is with me. Because of His victory on the cross, I can find my way through this battle, this brokenness and this dark world. I give it all to Jesus. I nail it all to His cross.

I GIVE IT ALL TO JESUS. I NAIL IT ALL TO HIS CROSS.

"Jesus, I relinquish my life, my will and my emotions to you. I apply the healing cross to my body. You are my peace and comfort. Amen."

The cross changes everything for me even though my circumstances haven't changed. I'm still facing a diagnosis I do not want and traveling down a path that I did not choose. But because of the cross, I have hope. In my suffering, God meets me. As I pick up the cross of my circumstances, Jesus places them on His back, and together we walk in victory through the darkness. Along the way, I encounter the gift of prayer from a hospital greeter, the gift of laughter from my sister, the gift of hope from my church, the gift of encouragement from my friends and the gift of strength from my family. Jesus continues to meet me in my suffering because He is with me. He knows what I need because He knows the depths of suffering. Despite my circumstances, I walk in victory. It's all because of the cross. We all need the cross.

Can you feel the suffering Savior with you in your waiting?

# MATTHEW 27:54-56

---

WHEN THE CENTURION AND THOSE WITH HIM WHO WERE GUARDING JESUS SAW THE EARTHQUAKE AND ALL THAT HAD HAPPENED, THEY WERE TERRIFIED, AND EXCLAIMED, "SURELY HE WAS THE SON OF GOD!" MANY WOMEN WERE THERE, WATCHING FROM A DISTANCE. THEY HAD FOLLOWED JESUS FROM GALILEE TO CARE FOR HIS NEEDS. AMONG THEM WERE MARY MAGDALENE, MARY THE MOTHER OF JAMES AND JOSEPH, AND THE MOTHER OF ZEBEDEE'S SONS.

# PRAYER

---

Dear God, Thank you for
sending your son Jesus to die
on the cross, and thank you for
raising Him to new life for my
sins. Forgive me for all of my
sins. I invite Jesus into my heart
to be my Savior. I want to follow
Him as Lord of my life from
this day forward.
Thank you again for the cross.
I'm overflowing with gratitude
in my heart for all you have done
for me. Thank you for healing
me with your stripes. Thank you
for the security of a home in
heaven. My salvation abounds.
Thank you for the cross Lord.
Amen.

## words worth repeating

NO MATTER WHAT SURROUNDS ME,
GOD IS WITH ME.

NO MATTER HOW HARD IT GETS,
I'M ALL IN FOR JESUS.

BECAUSE HE DIED, I AM FORGIVEN.

JESUS EXHAUSTED EVERYTHING
HARD THAT WE MIGHT EXPERIENCE
EVERYTHING GOOD FROM HIM.

HE COVERED EVERYTHING FOR
US ON THE CROSS.

I GIVE IT ALL TO JESUS.
I NAIL IT ALL TO HIS CROSS.

# Reflect

WHETHER ON
YOUR OWN OR
IN A COMMUNITY
OF OTHERS, ASK
THESE QUESTIONS
AND APPLY THEM
TO YOUR LIFE.

# Read

Matthew 26:14-27:66

Mark 14:27-15:47

Luke 22:47-23:56

John 18:1-19:27

*Are you facing something in your life where you need courage?*

*Are you all in for Jesus? Why or why not?*

*Sometimes you just need to sit with a friend in the hard. Who has sat with you in the hard?*

*Jesus suffered so that you and I might have life. Have you accepted Jesus' gift of eternal life?*

*What sin do you need to confess? He covered it!*

*Make a list of people in your life who need to hear the message of the cross, and begin to pray for them.*

*Take time to sit and relish in His cross-filled benefits: healing, provision, forgiveness, salvation, and acceptance. Which one do you need to receive the most right now? It's available to you.*

*How can you keep the cross close to your heart to serve as a daily reminder of what Jesus did for you? Perhaps a necklace, a list on the refrigerator, a sticky note on the dash, a bookmark in your Bible...*

# Reflect

WHETHER ON YOUR OWN OR IN A COMMUNITY OF OTHERS, ASK THESE QUESTIONS AND APPLY THEM TO YOUR LIFE.

# Read

Matthew 26:14-27:66

Mark 14:27-15:47

Luke 22:47-23:56

John 18:1-19:27

*Are you facing something in your life where you need courage?*

*Are you all in for Jesus? Why or why not?*

*Sometimes you just need to sit with a friend in the hard. Who has sat with you in the hard?*

*Jesus suffered so that you and I might have life. Have you accepted Jesus' gift of eternal life?*

*What sin do you need to confess? He covered it!*

*Make a list of people in your life who need to hear the message of the cross, and begin to pray for them.*

*Take time to sit and relish in His cross-filled benefits: healing, provision, forgiveness, salvation, and acceptance. Which one do you need to receive the most right now? It's available to you.*

*How can you keep the cross close to your heart to serve as a daily reminder of what Jesus did for you? Perhaps a necklace, a list on the refrigerator, a sticky note on the dash, a bookmark in your Bible...*

## FRESH PEAR SALAD
*Rachel Patton*

Rachel has taken many generous
roles in my life, and I am grateful
for her love and her Easter heart.
She is a mothering figure, a
confidant, a co-worker in Christ
and a dear friend. You will enjoy
her delicious pear salad all spring!

## SALAD

Boston leaf lettuce. *This is a light and airy lettuce. Wash and tear into pieces. Store in the refrigerator with a damp paper towel over the bowl until you're ready to toss.*

Sugared date bites. *These can be found in the bulk produce section or with the raisins. Make sure they are sugared!*

English walnuts

Blue cheese

Fresh ripe pear slices

## DRESSING

¼ cup canola oil

¼ cup white wine vinegar

2 Tbs. sugar

1 Tbs. Italian seasoning or spices such as basil, oregano, thyme from your cabinet

## DIRECTIONS

Toss all the salad ingredients together, and top with dressing.

*The Jerusalem School on Mt. Zion,*
*the school we attended*

*Skull Rock at The Garden Tomb*

*Spice shop
in Isreal*

*Doyle and
Jennifer,
newlyweds
in Isreal*

*Jennifer, a
Southern girl
at heart, hiking
on the road to
the Wedding at
Cana*

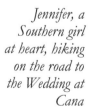

START WITH A QUICK
SENTENCE PRAYER

———

*Lord, I trust you
in the waiting.*

# The Burial

## A WAITING HEART

Hurry up and wait, that's how it feels lately. "We have all your results and will be scheduling you soon for a mastectomy," said the surgeon. I just wish I could go today and get this over with, but that is not possible. So I wait. I whisper to steady myself in the word of God, "Jennifer, be still and know…" Vacillating between bouts of courage and fear, nervousness and faith, I try to pray through this hurt. I dig into the foundation of my faith, searching for hope. I remember Nehemiah's words, "Do not grieve, for the joy of the Lord is your strength" (Nehemiah 8:10). I steel myself for joy on this journey no matter what comes next.

I am so thankful that I already have established routine times of meeting with the Lord. I go to my chair where everything is always situated on the little table: my pens,

YET THIS I CALL TO MIND AND THEREFORE I HAVE HOPE: BECAUSE OF THE LORD'S GREAT LOVE WE ARE NOT CONSUMED, FOR HIS COMPASSION NEVER FAILS. THEY ARE NEW EVERY MORNING; GREAT IS YOUR FAITHFULNESS. I SAY TO MYSELF, "THE LORD IS MY PORTION; THEREFORE I WILL WAIT FOR HIM."

*Lamentations 3:21-24*

highlighters, two or three Bible translations, devotionals and prayer journals. But where to start today? Today feels different. I'm in the waiting, and the problems of the past year seem smaller now. The heaviness of the pandemic, juggling indoor, outdoor and online services, helping Doyle at church, starting a radio show, managing a podcast, Doyle and I being sick with the virus, being away from family - all that stress seems far away compared to the reality of fresh medical news and the waiting.

Many days my routine starts very early in the morning, 4 a.m. to be exact. I'm up before the sun and my husband are even thinking about getting up. I choose to start my early mornings with prayer. Some days I like to start with reading, but not today. On this long, waiting day, I'm ready for a big chat with God because there is so much on my heart.

ON THIS LONG WAITING DAY, I'M READY FOR A BIG CHAT WITH GOD BECAUSE THERE IS SO MUCH ON MY HEART.

*Be still and know that I am God.* Psalm 46:10

After we talk for some time, I begin to worship and seek His presence. This rhythm - pray, worship, seek Him - is a rhythm I often follow, but this time it's different. This time I pray, worship and seek under the mounting pressure of the surgery and treatments that are looming on the horizon. *Peace, Lord, I'm searching for more of your peace. What else can I do in the waiting?* My stomach is still in knots. *Where is the peace? I need your peace, Lord.* I decide to sit with Him a bit longer, hoping He has more for me this morning, hoping He has so much more yet to pour over me as I sit in the waiting with my believing Easter heart.

I just love that I can tell the Lord all the numerous details that would bore anyone else, so I share everything with Him until I can't think of anything else to share. Slowly, I sense it. A subtle peace begins to surround me, and I breathe it in. I open my Bible, and the words give me life. The bread of life is my breakfast. I look at the clock and realize that I've been up for hours, sitting here with Jesus the entire time. Peace is flooding my spirit now, and I feel hope rising. Healing is in the air!

---

I PULL OUT MY JOURNAL AND BEGIN WRITING, COURAGE MOUNTING WITH EVERY STOKE OF MY PEN.

---

I wonder if this is what the women who sat at the foot of the cross did in the hours after Jesus' burial. Did they rally together or hide by themselves in their prayer closets? I wonder if they had appetites or if they felt continual waves of nausea as their minds replayed all of the trauma that they had witnessed. I'm sure they cried out to God, asking Him questions and seeking to understand what had happened and what was next. I trust that they still had a fraction of hope and faith, even if it was in threads. Mother Mary had seen water turned to wine, Mary Magdalene had been delivered of seven demons and the other mothers had walked with Jesus while their sons had witnessed many miracles. They knew the power of God.

Nevertheless, Jesus was dead. He was in the tomb. I've stood beside dozens of tombs, and it is never easy. Tombs, though filled with the body of the deceased, cause loved ones to feel so empty. Standing beside Jesus' tomb, in their grief and with their questions, the women still embraced God, the one true and living God of Abraham, Isaac and Jacob. Gripping tightly to their Easter believing hearts on a dark, wait-filled Saturday, they had a sliver of faith. Jesus taught them that if they had faith the size of a mustard seed anything was possible and any mountain could be moved. Did he really mean a faith that small? Did he really mean the impossible could be possible? What seems impossible in your life?

*What seems impossible in your life?*

"He replied, 'Because you have so little faith. Truly I tell you, if you have faith as small as a mustard seed, you can say to this mountain, 'Move from here to there,' and it will move. Nothing will be impossible for you'" (Matthew 17:20).

By the dark of night on the second day it must have been agonizing to wait and wait, but that is when the testaments are written and the resolutions of the heart are passed.

Stalled time in the midst of difficulty is when it is critical to be resolute in faith. During the most desperate times in our lives, we make a choice. We choose to go forward with Him or we choose not to. *"Mary Magdalene and Mary the mother of Joseph saw where he was laid"* (Mark 15:47). Of course they did! They were watching and waiting. They were loyal and involved as an example to you and to me. They chose to be with Him no matter what.

THEY CHOSE TO BE WITH HIM NO MATTER WHAT.

I'm not sure what you are waiting for. Maybe a baby to arrive? Maybe to conceive? Maybe a godly husband? A new job? A health outcome? What cry of victory do you want to shout during your waiting? Everyone waits. Some wait longer, and some wait harder. But we all have seasons of waiting.

In the middle of my waiting season, I commit to choosing Jesus when the waiting becomes too hard. Sometimes that choice is relatively easy, and sometimes that choice feels almost impossible. By deciding to choose Jesus before the going gets tough, I have given myself one less step toward finding Jesus while in the thick of the waiting.

*In the waiting, I choose:*

TO SEEK LIGHT IN THE DARKNESS

STRENGTH AND POWER IN THE MIGHTY LORD

A CALM, QUIET AND DISCIPLINED MIND OF PEACE

CONFIDENT COMPOSURE IN MY CALLING

AN ATTITUDE OF JOY AND A HEART OF
WORSHIP AND PRAISE

*In the waiting, I choose to say:*

"POWER THROUGH IT, ON HIS POWER."

"YOU HAVE A STRONG CONSTITUTION."

"TOMORROW'S NEW MERCIES WAIT FOR ME."

" I ADMIT I CANNOT DO THIS ON MY OWN;
I NEED THE LORD."

"GET SOME GRIT GIRL!"

The morning after Jesus' burial, during the day of "in between," I envision the women nervously pacing the house, wishing there was something they could do in the waiting. I imagine them gathering in the courtyard to talk. I imagine their conversations.

"What can we possibly do about all of this?" cries Mary.

"Well, I have an idea, spices! We can prepare those!" says the other Mary.

"Perfect, I will bring some fresh frankincense. It's my favorite spice, and I keep it on hand. We will take it to the tomb as an offering over Jesus' body," said Salome.

"Oh yes! This is a wonderful plan," said the other Mary, "I have plenty of aloe and myrrh! I'm going to go and gather it all together now, and I'll meet you at the tomb tomorrow morning. I'll check with Mary Magdalene to see what spices she has in the kitchen. Together this will be a beautiful anointing; it's the least we can do."

Salome piped in, "If we prepare His body, then He will be honored even in death."

*When the Sabbath was over, Mary Magdalene, Mary the mother of James, and Salome bought spices so that they might go to anoint Jesus' body (Mark 16:1).*

*On the first day of the week, very early in the morning, the women took the spices they had prepared and went to the tomb (Luke 24:1).*

---

IN THE WAITING WE OFTEN LOOK FOR
THINGS TO FILL OUR TIME AND MIND,
ANY POSSIBLE DISTRACTION SEEMS
TO OFFER MOMENTARY RELIEF.

---

I imagine that these women relished the time that it took to carefully choose, share and package the spices, but then what? When the house was quiet again and the Savior was still in the tomb, what then?

Another night started to fall. How would they sleep or eat when their hearts were so distraught? Their prayers were still unanswered, and their dreams appeared impossible. So they prayed, each in their own bed with quiet tears falling on their own pillow.

"God, can't you turn this around? How will Mary, His mother, ever be the same again after the horror we witnessed together? We need you now, right now in the midst of this waiting. Can you pour out your peace? The peace that passes understanding because nothing is making any sense right now. Please Lord, guard our hearts as we wait on you to do what only you can do. You are bigger, and you have all the power."

SO THEY PRAYED. THEY PREPARED. THEY STAYED VIGILANT. THEY KEPT GOING.

---

AND THE PEACE OF GOD, WHICH TRANSCENDS ALL UNDERSTANDING, WILL GUARD YOUR HEARTS AND YOUR MINDS IN CHRIST JESUS. *Philippians 4:7*

---

That group of close knit friends simply had to stand by and wait, lingering without knowing what the outcome would be. So they prayed. They prepared. They stayed vigilant. They kept going.

I wonder if they were tempted to numb out, grasp for some semblance of control or busily talk their way through the waiting? Does any of that sound familiar to you? As you wait for treatment results, a job offer, an overdue vacation, a healed hurt, a reunion with a loved one, an unfaithful spouse to repent or much needed rest from the relentless pain, how do you fill your time? Too often we reach for what will grant us the quickest relief only to soon find that it doesn't last. We reach for the food, alcohol, gossip, sleep, Netflix binge or anything else that distracts and numbs, and when it wears off, we discover the pain all over again.

*What if God wants to teach us something while we're in the waiting room?*

What if His ultimate goal is that we would trust Him completely even when we don't see the end result and even when the end result isn't what we prayed for.

God is at work during the wait, and we can be at work during the waiting as well.

Like the women at the cross, we too can pray, prepare, stay vigilant and keep going. When I found myself in a literal waiting room, in between tests, scans and results, I discovered that I was surrounded by women who were also in the waiting. God gave me eyes to see them as they also likely wondered, hoped, doubted and cried. As He softened my heart toward them, I prayed, asking God to meet them and to meet me in the waiting.

*Are you praying in the waiting?*

We can also prepare our hearts in the waiting. I love how the women gathered the spices. It was something practical that they could do together while they waited. For me, preparing in the waiting is reading God's word, strengthening my spirit with His truths as I wait.

Part of preparing is staying vigilant. Vigilance is turning off distractions such as certain types of media and avoiding things that steal my time and waste my energy. Instead, I created a routine that affords me more time with God, studying His word, talking with Him and writing in my journal. This vigilance allows me to better hear Him in the waiting.

Finally, I keep going. Though I am maintaining boundaries for my own health, I continue to serve my church, fellowship with encouraging friends and make time for Doyle and my family. Even though I am in the waiting, I know that God is still at work. I don't want to miss Him, and so I keep going, always looking to find Him through acts of service, fellowship and relationships.

No matter how long you are waiting, whether it be days, weeks, months, years or decades, God is at work. Pray, prepare, stay vigilant and keep going. God will meet you, even in the waiting.

This season of waiting reminds me of a couple that we met years ago in Israel.

Oh how we enjoyed a long hot day of hiking around Jerusalem to look at ruins and to find carvings or niches in buildings where perhaps we could learn a historical fact or pick up an old widow's mite coin in the dust. The city was stunning with an array of tan and golden limestone rocks with a backdrop of blue sky and lush, green trees. All throughout the city, artists crafted the most unique jewelry and pottery, and painters showcased their work, rich in color and symbolism from God's word with Hebrew lettering proclaiming His fame. Mounds of fresh oranges from Jericho and piles of figs and dates from the wilderness lined the streets. People wandered around from every tongue and tribe, literally from all over the world looking for Him. Israel is like coming home and exploring your hometown in a most unusual way. He is there. You sense it in the air you breathe, and the rocks cry out His praise. The Jerusalem streets are the streets Jesus and the disciples walked year after year, and their legacy is embedded throughout the place.

Nestled inside the Old City, a kind woman and her husband owned a small restaurant. I mean a little bitty shop with just enough room for three booths and a refrigerated case to sell hummus, salad and falafel - the best in town. She bought the fresh pita bread from an open oven around the corner in the Arab Quarter. It was divine.

So everyday, like clockwork, we passed by the sweet couple on our way back through the Old City to our apartment. The couple often waved at us to come in and eat. Usually we chatted briefly with them on the doorstep, and eventually, our friendship grew. I noticed that she wore the same dress every single day and her teeth needed a good cleaning. That seemed strange to me because, though small, their shop was very nice. Observing in my gut that something seemed out of place, I was prompted by the Holy Spirit to pray, "Lord, they are so kind to us, do they know You? What is their hidden story? Do they need something?" I quickly realized that God sent us on a people mission, and I needed to find out the couple's real story. Building trust was our first step, so we determined to stop at their shop frequently. Even if we couldn't buy food, we could at least chat and encourage them.

*My prayers increased.*

One day she seemed a bit panicky and asked me if I could babysit her kids. I agreed, wondering if this was the door to more information which could help us better reach them. Winding behind her on the cobblestone streets in a country far from home, I felt a bit uneasy as I followed her to her home. Yet I was determined to place some of God's love from my heart to hers, and so I continued. The dark apartment had only three rooms. Without any introductions or tour, she quickly left me with two kids and hurried out. I was reeling by the sight of no beds and only blankets and a thin mattress on the floor.

Her children were young, so we played games before they took their naps. When the children were asleep, I went into the kitchen. Opening a cabinet, I saw that it was empty. I opened another. Again, it was empty. Oh no, they have nothing here to eat. The third cabinet was also empty, except for bottles of liquor. His always red face and frequent grumpiness was beginning to make sense. "Thank you Lord. As hard as this is, now I know how to pray for them. Give us a door to their hearts, and protect the kids."

Over time, God answered our prayers. It began with her. As her heart softened, she began to pursue a relationship with Jesus. We continued to share Christ with them through gifts of clothing, eye glasses, encouragement and hope. She was lovely in the dresses, shoes and accessories I left for her. We prioritized their dignity, keeping what we knew about them to ourselves and keeping love at the center.

Though God softened her heart, his drinking and persistent grumpiness continued. So we continued in prayer. We prayed and we prayed and we prayed. Despite what seemed hopeless, we kept going.

We waited, and we prayed. Some days, it seemed impossible. His addiction had a hold on him. We prayed, we kept going and we waited some more. Day after day and year after year, we exchanged prayers for waiting.

Slowly we witnessed the cafe beginning to thrive and God becoming the center of their home. Though it wasn't a miraculous tah-dah that moved the impossible mountain, in time, and more importantly, in God's time, her husband began to change. Ultimately he too pursued Jesus. Our prayers were answered.

On every subsequent trip to Israel, we visited the couple, and we relished in what God did through the waiting. As we waited on God's timing, our faith grew because God drew us closer to Him. Nothing is impossible with God.

God is always worth the wait. He can do anything when we participate with Him, ask, notice and listen. Who in your life is worth the wait?

*God is always worth the wait. Who in your life is worth the wait?*

The couple from the small shop remind me that God has so much in store for us as we wait for Him. I'm also reminded that waiting is never without opportunity to seek Him despite what often feels like silence on His end. As I endure this season of waiting, I reach for ways to choose Jesus. I pray continuously. I prepare my heart through routine and discipline, and I stay vigilant. I keep going, grateful for every opportunity to share God's love with the people He has put in my life during this season. I guard my heart from Satan's schemes, prepare my heart for God's next step and posture my heart toward Jesus. I am not helpless in the waiting. On the contrary! God has gifted me an opportunity to hunger and thirst for His goodness, His provision and His love. That is worship in the waiting, and that is an Easter heart.

Whether you are in the waiting or on the other side, Jesus is king. What does it look like for you to worship Him through it all?

# PSALM 23:4

---

EVEN THOUGH I WALK

THROUGH THE DARKEST

VALLEY, I WILL FEAR NO

EVIL, FOR YOU ARE WITH

ME; YOUR ROD AND YOUR

STAFF, THEY COMFORT ME.

# PRAYER

---

Lord, I wait, I wait for you.
Lord, I long, I long for you.
Meet me here in the middle.
I stand firmly on the ground of
your word, believing you in faith
for the impossible.
Comfort me with your peace,
quiet me with your love and assure
me with your hope. Your mercies
are new every morning; great is
Thy faithfulness to me.
Amen.

*Pray this scripture over your own life:*
God, I can't do this burial of waiting on my own. I lean into your peace, and I ask you to protect my heart and my mind as I wait for you.

*And the peace of God, which transcends all understanding, will guard your hearts and your minds in Christ Jesus. Philippians 4:7*

## words worth repeating

I STEEL MYSELF FOR JOY
NO MATTER WHAT COMES NEXT.

I CHOOSE JESUS IN THE WAITING.

POWER THROUGH IT, ON HIS POWER.

GOD WILL MEET ME IN THE WAITING.

DESPITE WHAT SEEMS HOPELESS,
I WILL KEEP GOING.

NOTHING IS IMPOSSIBLE WITH GOD.

GOD IS ALWAYS WORTH THE WAIT.

# Reflect

WHETHER ON YOUR OWN OR IN A COMMUNITY OF OTHERS, ASK THESE QUESTIONS AND APPLY THEM TO YOUR LIFE.

# Read

## BURIAL

Matthew 27:59–61

Mark 15:46–47

Luke 23:53–56

John 19:39–42

*God is at work during the wait, and we can be at work during the waiting as well. What are you waiting for God to do?*

*How long have you been waiting? Choose God in the wait. Pray, prepare, stay vigilant and keep going.*

*Has God given you any assignments during the burial season? What are they?*

*Share with the Lord what you are learning while you wait. How are you trusting Him more?*

*What lessons have you learned from past experiences "in the middle"? How can you apply those to your life today?*

## EASY CHEESY
## POTATO CASSEROLE
*by Elaine Bartels*

Elaine is a humble woman who welcomes
Jesus into her life and home. Every Easter she
hosts an egg hunt and invites families to visit
her farm and experience the love of Christ.
Because of her Easter heart, she never stops
reaching out to the hurting, the lonely and
the lost. All of us can choose to reach more
people for Him with bold expressions of love
like Elaine.

## INGREDIENTS

2 bags of frozen homestyle hash brown cubes

1 extra-large can or two small cans of Campbell's Cream of Chicken Soup

½ cup of melted butter

8 ounce sour cream

2 cups shredded cheddar cheese

Salt & pepper to taste

## DIRECTIONS

Mix all together (then add the optional topping).

Bake at 350 degrees in the oven for one hour.

This goes great with the beef tenderloin and pear salad recipes in the previous chapters.

### OPTIONAL TOPPING

*Crush 2 cups cornflakes in a ziplock bag. Melt ½ stick of butter and drizzle over the top then bake.*

*The Garden Tomb*

*Old City wall of Jerusalem*

*Spices in a spice shop in Israel*

*Inside the Old City of Jerusalem*

*Jennifer at The Garden Tomb*

*Lord, Resurrect what
is dead within me.
Bring it to life.*

# The Resurrection

## A WORSHIPFUL HEART

*I*n the crushing, in the pressing, you are making new wine. Where there is new wine, there is new power. These lyrics flood my voice and soul all day as I do laundry, answer emails, return calls and make dinner. *Make me your vessel, make me an offering, make me whatever you want me to be.* I sing. I sing literally all the time. In the car, in the kitchen, in my office, in the shower and on my walks. I sing my way out of everything. I sing my way out of all the pits. Singing resurrects my soul. I sing to the Lord and worship Him. From early childhood, something about worshipful singing to God reminds me of how dear He is to me and the hope that is available to me everyday. I can't live without singing. If I ever stop singing, be concerned. I may not always have music, but I can sing and I can worship.

ALL THE NATIONS YOU HAVE MADE WILL COME AND WORSHIP BEFORE YOU, LORD; THEY WILL BRING GLORY TO YOUR NAME.

*Psalm 86:9*

It's only been a few short days since my diagnosis, and I already hate cancer. Quickly the days amount to a couple of weeks, and now I wait. I'm scheduled for surgery in four long weeks. It seems like I've been waiting forever on a resurrection from this situation in my life, and yet I have a peaceful assurance that it will come.

Sharing the news with a few family and friends is crushing, yet they offer me hope by surrounding me in their love and prayers. We all have people in our lives who are vital to our growth and well being, but ultimately, our encounters with God are what matter the most. It is His strength that we lean into when ours is gone. He is our living Savior and our best friend.

Can He really resurrect this body and situation of mine? The temptation is to think that maybe, just maybe a person can rescue me, but can God? For many years I substituted the quick fix of a friendship, my husband, my kids or family to be my all in all. It's easy to do. It's human to do. But my hope for you is that you will cross over to Jesus first and above all. Make a conscious decision to place God in the highest place of your life. By making Him the priority, you will begin to experience a life steeped in worship.

BY MAKING HIM THE PRIORITY, YOU WILL BEGIN TO EXPERIENCE A LIFE STEEPED IN WORSHIP.

What does it look like to live a life that worships God, and how do we get there? How do we get there when we have waited so long or walked through such pain?

*It all starts with the heart.*

No matter your pain, your circumstance, your burden or your path, no one can walk it for you - not your spouse, not your parents, not your surgeon, not your grandparents nor anyone else. A decision has to be made, choosing to give God your heart, your Easter believing heart. When we give God our heart and choose to place Jesus at the center of our life, we begin to release the grip on our pain, our circumstances, our burdens and our path. We begin to adjust our hearts toward finding the steady, calm and peace-filled Jesus who is always there for us amidst the chaos of our lives. This discipline, shift in attitude and commitment within the heart allows us to live a life of worship no matter what is going on around us and no matter what task we have before us.

*A worshipful heart is a heart that is centered on Jesus.*

A worshipful heart is a heart that is centered on Jesus. Singing to God is one way that we can live in worship to Him. Much like the first time you say out loud to someone that you love them, there is something significant about saying words of praise out loud to our God and King. There is power in that. Yes, we can worship at church in the community of believers.

That is an irreplaceable experience. But worship is not confined by the four walls of a sanctuary or to the stage at the front of a church.

*Worship is a posture of the heart.*

No matter what appears to be dying, I can live fully alive in praise. When I roll down the windows and join the band on my stereo in shouting and singing praise to God, I engage in worshipping Him along with the angels, saints and all of creation, a heavenly army together in worship. The enemy hates praise; he can't survive in the same atmosphere. So when we begin to sing, listen or actively participate in worship, the dead things come to life and the darkness has no choice but to flee.

WHAT DO YOU NEED RESURRECTED THAT ONLY GOD CAN DO?

What do you need resurrected that only God can do? Perhaps, in the good, the bad and the ugly, you sit before Him, at His feet and say, "Here I am, Lord. I choose to worship you for who you are: the creator of everything, the beginning and end of this world and my life. The healer, the sustainer and the keeper. I bow because you know my deeds, both good and bad, and I need your cleansing. I kneel because you are holy. I sing because written words aren't enough to proclaim your greatness. I sing from my diaphragm, and I pray that my worship pleases your heart. You promised that you love me unconditionally and always, and I bring you my offering today."

We all need to be resurrected, and only He can bring dead to life. He lived it so that we might know it. Can't you just feel the urgency of resurrection day? Hurry, hurry, hurry to the tomb! Sabbath rules were lifted, spices were packed and ready and hearts were still heavy from the past days' events. The women were eager to get to the tomb as soon as dawn broke. They showed up in anticipation of serving Jesus. In their minds, they knew He was dead, but in their hearts, they had hope.

With their Easter believing and hope-filled hearts, they arrived at the tomb to find the impossible. The stone had been rolled away. Not a rock, but a huge heavy tombstone had been moved. I love the loyalty of the disciples after such a public execution; they arrived at the tomb in hope. That is worship.

WE MUST NEVER LOSE HOPE OR FORGET THAT GOD IS A GOD WHO RESURRECTS, REDEEMS, RESTORES AND RENEWS.

His character is solid and unchanging. "Jesus Christ is the same yesterday and today and forever" (Hebrews 13:8). What are you holding onto, in hope, that only God can resurrect?

Just after sunrise, Mary Magdalene, Mary the mother of Joseph and Salome arrived with full arms brimming with spice gifts, faces still red and stained from tears and adrenaline pumping in anticipation for what was to come. They went from shock to shock because when they arrived, the stone had been rolled away and the tomb was empty. An angel in white sat next to an empty spot where Jesus' body should have been. They were freaking out in fear when the angel in white told them, "Do not be afraid, for I know that you are looking for Jesus, who was crucified. He is not here; he has risen, just as he said. Come and see the place where he lay" *(Matthew 28:5-6).*

As angels often did throughout scripture, the angel gave an instruction, "Then go quickly and tell his disciples. 'He has risen from the dead and is going ahead of you into Galilee. There you will see him'" (Matthew 28:7).

Their minds racing, the women were faced with the reality of the miracle they had hoped for, but could they find it in their hearts to believe? Life was coming at them fast. A flurry of activity, an empty tomb, questions and doubts and then they were faced with a choice. Could they believe what the angel said? Did they have enough faith to take action, quickly running to tell the others?

*An Easter heart is a believing heart.*

I'm impressed at their quick obedience to the angel. They must have prayed for this moment because they were the first to see, to run and to believe. Lord, may we be like them, just like them in their fierce faith and quick obedience!

Off they went, quickly running to immediately find Peter and John to bring them back to the tomb. Peter was the first to get up to go, but as they got closer to the tomb, John ran faster in an effort to be the first inside to see the empty tomb with his own eyes.

When John writes of this account in his gospel, he calls himself the disciple whom Jesus loved. Don't you just love that? Don't you just love the confidence that John had in the love of His Savior? What a great reminder of how much Jesus also loves you and me! I am Jennifer, the one whom Jesus loves. That feels good to say.

It was our first Easter as a couple. We lived in the Old City of Jerusalem in the Armenian quarter. Our house was a family's tool shed, but to me it was cozy and glorious. After all, I was with my dream guy studying God's word in the land of the Bible while living in daily expectation that the scriptures would resurrect, prune and transform all the dead spaces of my life.

LORD, MAY WE BE LIKE THEM, JUST LIKE THEM IN THEIR FIERCE FAITH AND QUICK OBEDIENCE!

We had a big day planned so we got up before daylight to get ready. We were going to experience Easter morning sunrise at the garden tomb. I was far from home for the first time in my life, and many miles from the American traditions of bunnies and baskets. Doyle and I walked out of the mini courtyard to the cobblestone streets, and much to my amazement, they were already packed with people.

We headed east with the crowd toward the Jewish quarter and turned left through the Cardo Maximus, walking and holding hands on the exact stone road from the time of Jesus, in anticipation of our favorite holiday.

The narrow streets began to tighten as crowds began to build. We were moving closer to Damascus Gate, one inch at a time. Soon the street was packed, literally people were side by side. There were people pressed against our arms and backs. I am five feet, ten inches tall, and even I was trying to stand on my tiptoes to see what was ahead. We were moving forward at a snail's pace. My chest tightened with a slight bit of panic as so many of us were jammed shoulder to shoulder.

Realizing I wasn't going anywhere fast, I started to sense the presence of God in my surroundings. The sun was beginning to rise, and the sky was a mix of pinks and blues as the limestone buildings glimmered.

---

ALL OF CREATION APPEARED TO SAY, "GOOD MORNING! YES, IT IS A SPECIAL DAY - IT IS RESURRECTION DAY!"

---

I calmed my spirit and began to look around. I had never witnessed people from all over the world within 20 feet of each other. I saw people from Greece, Egypt, China and more. Because of the large crowd, I was completely stopped at a standstill. I closed my eyes and listened. I heard French, Telugu, German and Spanish. I sensed the Holy Spirit nudging me to pay attention, and I felt utterly alive! The entire event was big, way bigger than anything I expected. I loved the purple flowing velvet robes of African priests and the long brown capes of Armenian monks. I could see the white headdresses of nuns who had traveled from England. I was surrounded by a variety of rich skin tones, a rainbow of vibrant clothing styles and a melody of different languages. What a sight to behold, all of us together and focused on the same mission.

OUR PLAN WAS TO GET TO THE EMPTY TOMB ON EASTER MORNING TO CATCH A GLIMPSE OF HEAVEN.

Our plan was to get to the empty tomb on Easter morning to catch a glimpse of heaven. We wanted to honor our king – King Jesus. We wanted to say thank you to Him, thank you for coming to this dusty old earth and praying for us, dying for us and rising again. We finally made it to the beautiful garden, and the smell of gardenia, jasmine and roses filled the air.

I could see the rock. I had a clear view of the outline of skull hill. Top archaeologists say that the actual location of the crucifixion was not right there, but that it was deeper into the heart of the old city walls. However, in that moment it didn't matter. We were there to celebrate Easter, we were there to worship and we were together. We were there in unity from every tongue and tribe, background and situation. Revelation 7:9 appeared across the screen of my mind. "After this I looked, and there before me was a great multitude that no one could count, from every nation, tribe, people and language, standing before the throne and before the Lamb. They were wearing white robes and were holding palm branches in their hands."

The full Israel sun began to blaze overhead as a reminder of the Son of God who so willingly came for us. Nothing could keep Him in the grave because the power of God raised Him up. Together we clapped, raised our hands and basked in His glory, coming together out of a desperate need to acknowledge Jesus. We stood and sang in awe of what He has done for us. "All the nations you have made will come and worship before you, Lord; they will bring glory to your name" (Psalm 86:9).

WHEN WE WORSHIP, WHETHER IN SONG, SPIRIT OR DEED, WE LONG TO BE RAISED UP AS WELL.

When we worship, whether in song, spirit or deed, we long to be raised up as well. Worship is everything. The power is in the cross; He defeated every enemy we face. We worship from the top of our lungs and from the bottom of our hearts, utterly amazed because there is victory over sin, over sickness, over poverty, over shame, over rejection and ultimately over death. The hope is in salvation. The hope is in heaven. The hope is in the comfort of knowing He is with us, forever.

As I organize my closet, moving my clothes to lower shelves so that they are easier to access as I begin my treatment process, I picture the resurrection in my mind. I am desperately waiting on Jesus to bring a resurrected healing to my physical body. My Easter heart is waiting, and my resurrected Savior gives me hope. As I fold shirts and place them on the shelf, I see my suffering Savior surrounded by every nation, tribe, people and language. I join them in worship. I sing. I begin to weep, still carrying my song through tears. I shout, and I sing. In between hangers and ironing. I wait, and I sing. I hope, and I sing. I trust, and I sing. Shoes neatly placed on the tiered rack. I wonder, pray and I sing. Laundry sorted and carried away in the basket. I sing, and I worship, and I sing.

THE HOPE IS IN THE COMFORT OF KNOWING HE IS WITH US, FOREVER.

I BELIEVE.

# BECAUSE HE LIVES

*William J. Gaither, 1971*

God sent His son, they called Him Jesus

He came to love, heal and forgive

He lived and died to buy my pardon

An empty grave is there to prove my

savior lives


Because He lives, I can face tomorrow

Because He lives, all fear is gone

Because I know He holds the future

And life is worth the living, just because

He lives

# MATTHEW 28:8-10

---

SO THE WOMEN HURRIED

AWAY FROM THE TOMB, AFRAID

YET FILLED WITH JOY, AND

RAN TO TELL HIS DISCIPLES.

SUDDENLY JESUS MET THEM.

"GREETINGS," HE SAID. THEY

CAME TO HIM, CLASPED HIS FEET

AND WORSHIPED HIM. THEN

JESUS SAID TO THEM, "DO NOT

BE AFRAID. GO AND TELL MY

BROTHERS TO GO TO GALILEE;

THERE THEY WILL SEE ME."

# PRAYER

---

Dear Jesus, There are so many
areas of my life that need
resurrection. Only you have the
power. Would you come now to
restore and renew those places
in my life. I am awed by the
beauty of your kingdom that is
filled with people from every
background and nationality.
Thank you! I want to obey you
quickly and run to you like
Mary, John and the others did. I
want to see miracles and live in
your hope. I believe.
Amen

MEMORIZE

*I am the resurrection and the life. The one who believes in me will live, even though they die; and whoever lives by believing in me will never die. Do you believe this?"…Jesus* John 11:25-26

# words worth repeating

I MAY NOT ALWAYS HAVE MUSIC, BUT I CAN SING AND I CAN WORSHIP.

I CHOOSE TO GIVE GOD MY EASTER BELIEVING HEART.

I LEAN INTO HIS STRENGTH WHEN MINE IS GONE.

THEY KNEW HE WAS DEAD, BUT THEY HAD HOPE.

GOD IS A GOD WHO RESURRECTS, REDEEMS, RESTORES AND RENEWS.

AN EASTER HEART IS A BELIEVING HEART.

I AM (INSERT YOUR NAME), THE ONE WHOM JESUS LOVES.

# Reflect

# Read

Matthew 28:1-10

Mark 16:1-8 & 9-14

Luke 24:1-44

John 20:1-29

*Believe through prayer, with an Easter heart, that God can resurrect the dead things in your life. What do you need resurrected that only God can do?*

*Choose to worship God for who He is. Worship by bowing down, kneeling before Him and living a life of humility and praise. Close your eyes and sense His presence.*

*Find time everyday to sing, and praise God for who he is and what he has done in your life. Is singing, praise and worship part of your routine? How can you incorporate more time in worship into your life?*

*Take a moment and imagine heaven. Picture all the people who love God, from all around the world, bowing and praising Him. Place yourself in this image.*

*Are you making plans now to celebrate the resurrection? How can you make it extra special this year?*

## PIMENTO CHEESE
## FRENCH BRAIDED BREAD

This is a well used traditional recipe passed down from my wonderful mother-n-love, Betty Jackson. She always sets the most gorgeous spring tables with china, mint green or pale yellow glasses, fresh flowers and ironed napkins. I cherish all the deep belly laughs around her table, the many prayers and the deep discussions with the family about everything happening in the world around us. She is a true hostess, mother and grandmother whose Easter heart places great value on time with family, especially at Easter.

This recipe makes two large beautiful braids of bread. It takes time, but the effort is worth it. I always make it in between my Easter preparations: cleaning, laundry and table setting. I simply reheat it on Easter day.

## INGREDIENTS

1 ½ packages of quick rise yeast
4 ½ cups Gold Medal self rising flour
1 ½ cups milk 2% or higher
2 Tbs. of sugar
1 ½ tsp. salt
1 large egg
8 ounce carton of pimento cheese

## DIRECTIONS

Combine yeast and two cups of flour. Heat together
the milk, sugar and salt until warm (1 minute 20 seconds
in microwave). Add to the dry mixture, and gently stir.
Add egg and pimento cheese. Beat at a low speed for 30
seconds; scrape sides of bowl. Beat at medium speed for 3
minutes. By hand stir in enough of the remaining flour to
make a stiff dough. Turn out onto a well floured surface (I
always flour my hands before starting). Knead by hand 8-10
minutes until smooth. Place in a greased bowl, cover with
a bit of oil and wrap the bowl tight with saran wrap. Cover
with a clean dish cloth, and let rise until doubled in size.

Punch down. Divide the dough into 6 pieces, cover and let
rest again for 10 minutes.

Preheat the oven to 375 degrees, and grease a baking sheet
with spray Pam or oil. Roll each piece into a roll about 15"
long, and shape into two long braids. Cover again with
a dish cloth, and let rise until doubled in size (about 30
minutes). Bake for 15-20 minutes, and brush with melted
butter when fresh. *Enjoy!!*

*Tombstone that was rolled away*

*The neighborhood in the Old City*

*Jennifer doing laundry at school in Jerusalem*

*Jennifer in the apartment in Israel*

*Jennifer and Doyle, newlyweds in Israel, 1991*

START WITH A QUICK
SENTENCE PRAYER

———

*Jesus, Thank you
for your living hope.*

## 6

# The Living Hope

### A VICTORIOUS HEART

If not for Doyle's parents, I don't know that we ever would have visited Israel, let alone lived there. When my in-laws were transformed by the saving grace of the cross, the powerful truth of the gospel changed everything in their lives. Their eyes were opened to the undeniable history that spans the pages of scripture, and because of their Easter hearts, they longed to see for themselves the physical place where Jesus was born and where he lived, walked and was crucified.

The Jacksons first visited Israel in 1969, and ever since they have been determined to see that everyone in the family experiences the Holy Land. To this day, Doyle's parents continue to share with others the victory and hope that is in Jesus, whether it be in Tennessee, Ohio,

MAY THE GOD OF HOPE FILL YOU WITH ALL JOY AND PEACE AS YOU TRUST IN HIM, SO THAT YOU MAY OVERFLOW WITH HOPE BY THE POWER OF THE HOLY SPIRIT.

*Romans 15:13*

Israel or anywhere in between.

We flagged down a cab and together jumped inside. Doyle's dad was taking us to one of his favorite restaurants on the road to Emmaus. We sat outside eating a delightful dinner while reveling in the balmy warm weather with orange blossom flowers cascading over dozens of pretty limestone cafes in front of a stunning orange sunset sky.

As we fellowshipped over a meal of fresh fish, vegetables, olives and grape leaves, we talked about Jesus. We talked about what life was like before and after Jesus. We laughed and shared about the people, experiences, friends and family we have shared Jesus with over the decades. Doyle's dad shared about how a man once asked if he would pray for him to be free of his cigarette addiction. Doyle's dad had prayed, and the man was immediately set free, delivered of a lifelong habit in Jesus' name. Story after story, we shared of the goodness of our miraculous God.

In that Emmaus setting, feasting and fellowshipping with beloved family and followers of Jesus, there was no way to deny the reality that Jesus' death and resurrection remains our victory and living hope.

All of us, in addition to hundreds of others, have experienced a similar Emmaus feast in Israel because of the Jacksons' invitation and belief that seeing the land of the Bible brings Jesus to life.

Can you imagine what an opportunity the disciples were given to walk the Emmaus Road with Jesus, to talk and eat with the risen Savior and king? They physically spent time with Jesus after He rose from the dead. I think they must have clung to those memories for strength as they carried the gospel for many miles and across roaring seas and ultimately to the ends of the earth until their very last breath. The point of Emmaus is that the journey continues. The miracle of knowing Jesus is not confined to that moment in history or a road in Israel. Rather, the walks, meals, healings and deliverances with Jesus continue on, so long as we can see.

*Lord, open our eyes to see you.*

The great thing about the Emmaus story is that we all get caught in the journey, the walk of life. Jesus is with us, and when we fail to see that, He isn't upset with us. Instead He loves us enough to be with us and to walk with us through life. Quietly His Holy Spirit opens our eyes. We see that we have been walking with the risen Jesus longer than we imagined. He is always with us in a very real way.

HE IS ALWAYS WITH US IN A VERY REAL WAY.

This is what happened to me as I walked the streets of Jerusalem. I realized that the risen Lord was with me in a powerful new way. It was like discovering hidden treasure in a field. You are walking with Jesus this Easter season. I am walking with him too, and we simply have to ask him to open our eyes. Help me see you Lord!

"Then their eyes were opened and they recognized him, and he disappeared from their sight. They asked each other, 'Were not our hearts burning within us while he talked with us on the road and opened the Scriptures to us?'" (Luke 24:31-32).

Jesus, the risen and resurrected Jesus, was with them, and they did not recognize Him. I wonder how often they later reflected on that day and gained strength from remembering that they were not alone because even though they did not realize it, Jesus had been with them.

*We are never alone.*

The road to Emmaus reminds me of another surprising Jesus encounter. While He was at the well to draw water, a woman met Jesus. Similar to the disciples on the road to Emmaus, she did not recognize Him. She did not know that she was speaking with the Messiah. He asked her for a drink, and then He offered her an unexpected gift, a no cost life hack. He offered her living water.

*Jesus answered her, "If you knew the gift of God and who it is that asks you for a drink, you would have asked him and he would have given you living water. Everyone who drinks this water will be thirsty again, but whoever drinks the water I give them will never thirst. Indeed, the water I give them will become in them a spring of water welling up to eternal life" (John 4:10, 13-14).*

In that moment she faced a choice. If she chose to follow him daily, to share his hope with everyone she meets and to live under his direction and care, then and only then, she would drink from the well that never runs dry. That same well of living water is offered to you and to me. It is wide and deep, and it is full of promises for freedom and new life. To have an Easter heart is to know that you live every day with the risen Jesus, and because He lives, you can face tomorrow.

---

THIS WOMAN HAD NEVER MET A MAN
WHO GAVE AWAY HOPE SO FREELY.

---

Living fully in the hope of Jesus changes everything. It changes the way we think, what we do and who we spend time with. Living in victory ignites a life of praise, worship, prayer and service. Because of Jesus' sincere interest in me, I am compelled to give back to my Savior who rose for me, and I am inspired to share with others so that they too can know a life of hope.

Living in hope is a lifestyle of humility, bowing low and laying down our coats, then standing up with a palm branch in hand to praise Him. It's a lifestyle of giving back literally with our treasure and giving our very being to others in hopes that they too might know Him.

Service has been the centerpiece of Easter for many years at our home church, The Church Next Door. Grabbing the little red wagon and my two blonde boys, my family and I set out on a mission throughout Thornapple Grove, a nearby neighborhood. The wagon was packed full with mugs, candy and invitations to our church's Easter celebration. From house to house we invited everyone who would listen to our prompting, and so many of them did. We were so excited for our first egg hunt, and God must have been excited too. Fifty young families showed up to find eggs and receive the good news of Jesus.

Each year, the Easter hunt grew a little bigger. It grew and it grew, and one spring I searched for the largest tent that I could find in Columbus, Ohio. Under a circus-size tent, we coordinated hayrides, egg hunts, animal visits, photo ops and so much more for an anticipated 5,000 people. God grew our humble invitation one hundredfold, and it was exhilarating as we prepared to share the hope of Jesus with our neighbors.

When it was finally the day of the big tent set up, we woke to discover the most horrific weather outside. Pouring rain and pockets of mud filled the 34 acre field where we were planning to set up the festivities. I traipsed across the entire 34 acres for two hours, begging the event company to set up our tent despite the conditions. They said it simply would not work.

I had spent weeks planning and thousands of church dollars, not to mention, we invited every soul we could find within a 15 mile radius.

*Yet the rain would not relent. It poured.*

My mind was set: It just had to work. God surely wouldn't fail us now. It was all for Him and for His glory. Reluctantly the tent crew finally agreed on a location where they could set up, but the challenge was far from over.

Determined to have our annual event, we prayed fervently, "Lord, we just want to honor you in this holy season. So many people in our community have never heard of you or witnessed your love in action. We have served you and worked so hard preparing for this moment for months, and the plans seem to be failing, help us! We thought for sure that this was your plan to share the good news to the children and families on the west side of the city. If so, please show us what to do. So much rain and water is ruining everything, everywhere."

Not long after our prayer of desperation, my oldest son, Aaron, had an idea. At the time he worked for a farmer and decided to purchase and haul three large wagons full of straw to the church. My younger son, Peter, and the men of the church showed up to spread the straw under the tent. It was an all day project. In addition to the wagons of straw, they brought their shop vacuums and literally vacuumed the muddy water up and out of our way. God provided!

The next morning, the morning of the event, the sun came out in all her glory. After we were nearly wiped out by the rain and mud, we finally woke up to gloriously sunny and dry weather. After the event company initially said we could not set up a tent, and after 34 acres of mud nearly swallowed us whole, God was making a way. That day thousands of people poured onto campus with little ones in tow, brimming with excitement. Every hour on the hour, hundreds by hundreds, we hunted 40,000 eggs, sang songs, praised God, watched Easter stories and ate cotton candy until every heart was content and full with the love of God. We were living and celebrating Jesus, our living hope.

---

WE WERE LIVING AND CELEBRATING
JESUS, OUR LIVING HOPE.

---

Finally home after the exhausting festivities, three glorious Palm Sunday services and a week of service prep, it was time for the grand finale: our church's four Easter Sunday services. God outdid Himself. The celebrations were beyond beautiful! Giant flower pots of yellow forsythia and lilies lined the stage, children danced and sang, and violins and trumpets played with the choruses of our worship team. My husband preached his heart out with the care that only a loving pastor can bring to a seeking crowd of hungry church goers. It was a hope-filled weekend that I will never forget.

Though worn down and tired, I was bound and determined for my little family to still experience our own personal Easter celebration. As a pastor's family, I never wanted my kids to feel like they got their parents' leftovers. So I pressed on toward the prize of creating a special Easter memory, an Emmaus type experience, for our sweet family of four.

I set the table, remembering the words of my grandmother, "use your china or it will never get used." I ironed cloth napkins and used the good silverware. We cooked, baked and prepared our favorite recipes and Easter treats. It was a table and feast set for a king in celebration of our risen King.

Filling our table with beauty and delicious food is a memory that I cherish in my heart. As I look ahead to this Easter, I know it will be different. My boys are grown and both married. We are still living with a global pandemic, and I am facing a new diagnosis and the treatments that come with it. Though I don't know who will be around the table this Easter, and though we won't be able to host thousands of families for a rain or shine egg hunt, I am confident that the hope of Jesus will be the centerpiece of our celebration no matter how it unfolds.

IT WAS A HOPE-FILLED WEEKEND THAT I WILL NEVER FORGET.

IT WAS A TABLE AND FEAST SET FOR A KING IN CELEBRATION OF OUR RISEN KING.

THE LIVING HOPE OF JESUS IS NOT ONLY
WHAT EASTER IS ALL ABOUT, IT IS WHAT
YOUR LIFE AND MY LIFE IS ALL ABOUT.

Because of the cross and resurrection, because of everything that Jesus has done and continues to do for His people, because of God's great and mighty love for each of us, we have the gift of knowing victory and living in hope.

As I move forward in my own healing journey, I know that I am not alone. Jesus has been with me every step of the way. I have felt His loving kindness in the medical staff that I have met, the prayers of friends and family and the strength He continues to give me through it all. One thing I don't only believe but firmly know is that God's character never changes. He is the Healer. He is my healer, and He is your healer. No matter what report you may have been given, remember that God's word is even better and the risen Savior is the best news of all.

"By his wounds you have been healed" (1 Peter 2:24). That is my prayer for all of us. Remember you are dearly loved. No matter what you face, no matter what pain you have endured and no matter the hardship that is ahead, you can know a life of abundant love, grace, mercy and hope because you have the risen Jesus and because you believe, this Easter and always.

# JOHN 4:7-10

---

WHEN A SAMARITAN WOMAN CAME TO
DRAW WATER, JESUS SAID TO HER, "WILL
YOU GIVE ME A DRINK?" (HIS DISCIPLES HAD
GONE INTO THE TOWN TO BUY FOOD.) THE
SAMARITAN WOMAN SAID TO HIM, "YOU
ARE A JEW AND I AM A SAMARITAN WOMAN.
HOW CAN YOU ASK ME FOR A DRINK?"
(FOR JEWS DO NOT ASSOCIATE WITH
SAMARITANS. JESUS ANSWERED HER, "IF
YOU KNEW THE GIFT OF GOD AND WHO IT IS
THAT ASKS YOU FOR A DRINK, YOU WOULD
HAVE ASKED HIM AND HE WOULD HAVE
GIVEN YOU LIVING WATER."

# PRAYER

---

Dear Jesus,
You have given everything for
me; I want to give everything
for you.  Show me where to
serve, how to do it and who
needs the most attention.  I
cannot do this on my own
strength, but instead, I will trust
in Yours.  You are my living
hope, and I choose to sacrifice
and give my time back to You.
You have died for me, and now
I want to live in hope for You.
Amen

## MEMORIZE

*May the God of hope
fill you with all joy and
peace as you trust in him,
so that you may overflow
with hope by the power of
the Holy Spirit.*

*Romans 15:13*

## words worth repeating

BECAUSE OF JESUS, WE ARE
NEVER ALONE.

AN EASTER HEART CHOOSES
JESUS EVERYDAY.

LIVING FULLY IN THE HOPE OF JESUS
CHANGES EVERYTHING.

LIVE AND CELEBRATE JESUS,
OUR LIVING HOPE.

THE LIVING HOPE OF JESUS IS
WHAT ALL OF LIFE IS ABOUT.

# Reflect

WHETHER ON YOUR OWN OR IN A COMMUNITY OF OTHERS, ASK THESE QUESTIONS AND APPLY THEM TO YOUR LIFE.

# Read

WOMAN AT
THE WELL

John 4:1-42

THE ROAD
TO EMMAUS

Luke 24:13-32

*An Easter heart lives each day with the risen Jesus, giving us strength for each day. By choosing to live in hope, how might that change your life?*

*How has the Holy Spirit opened your eyes to Jesus? When you look back on your life, can you see how He was with you even when you didn't realize it at the time?*

*Specifically, how are you going to serve Jesus in your church or community?*

*Who in your life needs the hope of Jesus? Pray for them now.*

*Who can you share the living hope with this Easter? How might you serve them?*

*What aspect of your life is most desperate for the living hope of Jesus to shine through?*

## CLASSIC COCONUT CAKE
*from Southern Living*

All of the recipes in this book are special to me because they
originated from someone who has shown me an Easter heart.
The coconut cake is no different. Though the coconut cake
recipe does not originate from one specific person, it is a cake
that represents the gift of Easter from so many neighbors,
friends and church members throughout the years. No matter
the occasion, when I am with our family in the South, we
almost always enjoy a gift from a loved one, a coconut cake.
Enjoy this recipe with your own family, or give to a loved one
as a gift and an extension of your Easter heart.

# INGREDIENTS

### COCONUT CAKE
3 cups all-purpose flour
1 tsp. baking powder
½ tsp. salt
2 2/3 cups sugar
1 cup shortening
½ cup butter, softened
1 cup milk
2 tsp. coconut extract
5 large eggs
1 (6-oz.) package frozen
flaked coconut, thawed
coconut shavings, for
garnish

*Color the frosting
green like grass and
add jelly beans to
decorate for Easter.*

### COCONUT FILLING
1 cup sugar
2 Tbs. all-purpose flour
1 cup milk
2 large eggs, lightly
beaten
1 (6-oz.) package frozen
flaked coconut, thawed
½ tsp. vanilla extract
½ tsp. coconut extract

### WHIPPED CREAM FROSTING

1 ½ cups heavy cream
3 Tbs powdered sugar
1 ½ Tsp coconut extract

# DIRECTIONS

## MAKE THE COCONUT CAKE.
*Preheat oven to 400°F. Grease and flour 4 (9-inch) round cake pans.*

Beat first 7 ingredients at medium speed with an electric mixer until well blended. Add extract, beating well. Add eggs, 1 at a time, beating until blended after each addition. Stir in flaked coconut. Pour batter into prepared pans.

Bake at 400°F for 20 minutes or until a wooden pick inserted in center comes out clean. Let cool in pans on wire racks 10 minutes. Remove from pans to wire racks, and cool completely (about 1 hour).

Meanwhile, reduce oven temperature to 350°F. Arrange coconut shavings in a single layer in a shallow pan. Bake, stirring occasionally, 8 to 10 minutes or until toasted.

## MAKE THE COCONUT FILLING.
Cook first 4 ingredients in a large saucepan over medium-low heat, whisking constantly, 12 to 15 minutes or until thickened and bubbly. Remove from heat, and stir in coconut and extracts. Let cool completely (about 30 minutes).

## MAKE THE WHIPPED CREAM FROSTING.
Beat all ingredients at high speed with an electric mixer until stiff peaks form.

## ASSEMBLE:
Spread Coconut Filling between layers of cake, leaving a 1-inch border. Spread Whipped Cream Frosting on top and sides of cake. Sprinkle toasted coconut on top of cake, pressing gently to adhere.

1. Napkin
2. Salad Fork
3. Dinner Fork
4. Dinner Plate
5. Salad Plate
6. Soup Bowl
7. Dinner Knife

8. Tea Spoon
9. Soup Spoon
10. Salad Knife
11. Bread Plate
12. Butter Knife
13. Dessert Knife
14. Dessert Spoon

15. Cake Fork
16. Water Goblet
17. Red Wine Glass
18. White Wine Glass
19. Tea/coffee saucer
20. Tea/coffee cup
21. Guest card

I hope you enjoy this simple table map, and it adds something special to your Easter celebration. With a little extra effort, you will enjoy great food across a gorgeous table as you indulge in tangible time with your loved ones and celebrate the Risen King! He is Risen! He is Risen indeed!

*A group in the Judean wilderness near the pathway of the Good Samaritan*

*Israel tour group on the steps to the temple where Jesus taught*

*Doyle and Jennifer in Israel*

*Israeli salad*

*Jennifer with Doyle's parents*

*This 6-chapter devotional invites you to*

## DISCOVER THE RESURRECTED JESUS AS YOU LEAN INTO HIS LIVING HOPE.

Through these pages you will discover that an Easter heart is not a heart that busies oneself with bunnies and baskets. Rather an Easter heart is a heart that is humble, desperate, suffering, waiting, worshipful and victorious. An Easter heart is a heart that believes in Jesus.

Travel with the author to Israel, and discover the glory of historical truth. Learn from the women who were with Jesus during his final days, and learn from the author as she shares her personal account of meeting Jesus in the midst of an unexpected healing journey.

*There is so much hope in an Easter heart. Do you believe?*

JENNIFER JACKSON is devoted to Jesus and leading others to walk with Him. She loves mentoring women by helping them discover God no matter where they are in life. Jennifer and her husband have spent the last 29 years working in full time ministry and sharing God's love with everyone they meet. They live in Columbus, Ohio and have two grown sons and wonderful daughter-in-laws.

**www.jennifer-jackson.org**